DIARY OF A BABY—

An African Village Life
As Told By A Baby!

DIARY OF A BABY—

An African Village Life
As Told By A Baby!

Robert Peprah-Gyamfi

Perseverance Books

Published by Perseverance Books
Loughborough
Leicestershire
UK

info@peprah-gyamfi.org
www.peprah-gyamfi.org

ISBN: 978-1-913285-24-1

TABLE OF CONTENTS

FOREWORD

A psychiatrist who used hypnosis to regress his patients back to their beginnings once told me that often he was able to help his patient recall his or her awareness as far back as the womb! In fact, he told me that the baby makes its own decision when to turn into the birth position! So then, perhaps it is not so far-fetched to imagine the baby's experience of birth—and the early days or years, following the birth. And this is exactly what our author has done! The author in fact is a medical doctor, and in this book his imagination has served as the baby's mouthpiece of a typical rural Ghanaian baby's early experiences.

It is a very clever and effective literary approach, and especially valuable as he has used a baby from his own native Ghana to tell the story of a typical African baby's experience of being born into a very poor remote rural village. The baby is the book's centre of consciousness, and of great interest not only to African readers, some of who may be familiar with the circumstances of coming to terms with an impoverished African experience, but particularly, I should think, for a Western reader, whose eyes are hereby opened to the penurious circumstances and challenges that face the new arrival.

What makes the reading of this book so delectable is the author's adoption (on the baby's part) of a fairly erudite and confidential style, with unconscious touches of humour and irony! The baby's initial addiction for and fascination with the pleasurable satisfying quality of breastmilk is a liquid thread that flows irresistibly through the early memories of our baby!

I cannot stop repeating how tasty mother's breast milk is! How does she manage to cook such a delicious meal in her body? I can only wonder. Anyway, I am now filling my tummy with as much breast milk as I can lay hold on!

And there's the baby's unfailing strategy to achieve his aims, whether it be a demand for more delicious breast milk (the panacea for all problems) or the relief from pain or irritation of mosquitoes or loud noises of farm animals, which is to cry like mad! One is aware of the many causes of pain in his cultural and social context, whether it be the cutting of tribal markings on the cheeks, or the pain from the bursting of boils, or the fear of the dark—the strategy *always* works, even if an increase in volume or a frantic waving of arms and legs are required! The confiding manner ensures the reader's sympathy.

The book has a much deeper purpose than the simple sharing of a new-born baby's experiences, however. The author is a great fighter in the arena of social reform, and his polemical purpose is swallowed as naturally and easily as the baby swallows his mother's breast milk! The urgent problems of poverty are very much in the foreground—the lack of immediate medical attention, the long potholed roads that have to be travelled in packed vehicles, to reach a hospital to save a baby's life, are always present. And as the baby gets older, in his fourth year as his consciousness or awareness expands, he begins to wonder about going to school—which he yearns to do. Why indeed is there no prospect of schooling for him when his well-to-do cousin in the city goes to kindergarten and plays with fancy factory-manufactured toys? Since Independence the Government has promised free schooling for every child, urban or rural; but, as the book reaches its end, the echoing cry is—but when?

But let me not give away the fascinating—or disturbing—circumstances of the baby's story. It is an arresting story, indeed a heart-warming story, that will place the reader right in the centre, the very essence, of a Ghananian village, or compound, where there are no fences, no walls between the very basic homes, where the communal farm animals wander freely, and where the problems and needs are shared in keeping with the essential African impulse to share and help one another.

Charles Muller

MA (Wales), PhD (London), DEd (SA), DLitt (UFS)

ACKNOWLEDGEMENTS

My heartfelt thanks go to God Almighty, for imparting the wisdom needed to write this book.

Rita, my wife, together with our children Karen, David, and Jonathan, also deserve my thanks and appreciation for their support and encouragement, which enabled me to persevere to the successful conclusion of this work.

I am also grateful to Dr Charles Muller for carrying out the editorial work and for writing the foreword.

YEAR 1

1A

THE ARDUOUS JOURNEY TO PLANET EARTH

Hey! What's going on here? Everything surrounding me seems to be moving in angry waves. It's strange, really strange. Since I made my home in this enclosure, I have experienced periodic jerks, shakes, tremors. They have on the main been short-lived and nothing of the intensity I am subjected to now!

For God's sake, whoever or whatever is behind this unbearable state of affairs? Could you please leave me in peace!

My complaining seems to have had some effect! Thankfully the commotion has ceased and calm has been restored to my environment. That's heartening; I shall retire to rest for a while.

Oops! My relief has been short-lived. Indeed, the calm has turned out to be just a momentary calm in the midst of the storm, for turbulent waves have returned with a vengeance! My goodness, if only someone would be kind enough to tell me what's going on here! Instead, I am kept in the dark!

The pressure meanwhile has increased in intensity. Apparently, someone has resorted to what can aptly be described as terror tactics to evict me from my safe abode. Should that indeed be the case, then one could rightly ask the question: fairness, where art thou?

Having been granted permission to reside here over the last several months, fairness would indeed require that I am served a notice of eviction in advance—at least a few if not several weeks beforehand.
But lo and behold, without any prior notice, I am all of a sudden being forcefully, even violently expelled from my residence!

What am I to do? Well, I've decided to stay put! If whoever instigated this unilateral action did not deem it necessary to give me prior notice of their intentions, then I am not obliged to be courteous to them. In short—I'm going nowhere!

I'm working out an effective strategy to counter their efforts—I'm pressing my back firmly against the wall supporting me! To add further force to the backward thrust, I am also stretching my two legs firmly to the wall facing me. That way, I hope to neutralize the force trying to propel me forward.

Wow! The strategy seems to be working! After mounting a fierce resistance to counter their attempt to push me out of my safe refuge, whoever or whatever is behind it seems to have given up – out of exhaustion, no doubt! So, for now, calm has returned to the 'battlefield'. For now, at least, I can congratulate myself for a job well done!

The resistance has taken its toll on me though—yes indeed, I feel so drained, so exhausted. My muscles are aching, aching badly. I'll take advantage of the calm to rest for a while, to regenerate my energy. I hope this is the end of the matter with the attempted forced eviction.

I might have fallen asleep—no idea for how long. What is certain though is that I've been brutally torn out of my sleep by—are they vibrations; are they waves? My immediate surroundings are in a real state of agitation; I can feel sustained pressure pressing on me from all directions! It appears I'm being literally squeezed to death! This is beyond anything I have ever experienced. Goodness me! How is this terrifying encounter going to end?

*

Hey! I have experienced a sudden horizontal propulsion! The thrust was so strong and unexpected it has pushed me a good deal forward. I would have been propelled even further down the road had it not been for what appears to be a wall. Ach, my head is hurting from the impact with what appears to be a 'brick wall'. Very lucky my delicate head was not crushed to pieces in the process.

It appears I have ended up at the very end of a cul-de-sac. With no clear direction to turn, I'm at the mercy of the sustained pressure propelling me forward. I have to find a way of saving my life; remaining passive and doing nothing will most likely result in my head being crushed into a pulp.

Though it's dark all around me, I have figured out that the passage through which I am being propelled is not a dead-end street, as I thought. To my relief, I have established it makes a bend to the left. I will thus have to make a left-turn so as to follow the course of the path.

On second thoughts, it has dawned on me that such a step could end up facilitating my expulsion. Still, I will opt for that option; it boils down in my view to sticking to the lesser of two evils.

*

I am not immediately able to put my plan into action. For whatever reason, the force that I just referred to has abruptly subsided. The saying has it that it takes two to tango. Under the circumstances, I have no option but to put my plans on hold for now. I am taking advantage of the tranquil situation to rest awhile. I need time to regenerate my strength.

On the basis of my experience of the force acting on me just now, I can only assume the quiet will not last for long; and that is exactly what has turned out to be the case. Indeed, hardly had I closed my eyes to sleep than the propelling force returned—with a vengeance! I took advantage of the situation to put the plan I just referred to into action—and it worked! So for now I have been pushed leftwards along the brick wall.

I have taken advantage of a decrease in the pressure acting on me to quickly examine my immediate surroundings. Though I initially thought I was imagining things, there seems indeed to be a ray of light not very far ahead of me! What then can be the source of the light? I can only wonder!

Once again, I can feel the effect of the thrust acting on me. Slowly but surely, I am being gradually pushed forward, towards what without doubt now appears to be a source of light.

Alas! My head has emerged out of the tunnel! Eh! I can sense a change in temperature. My head, which is outside the enclosure I have already referred to, feels the outside heat which appears scorching, whereas the rest of my body continues to feel the way it has always felt.

There is a standstill here; nothing is happening! Indeed, for a while nothing has been happening—there is indeed no movement or activity at all.

Initially, I thought once the pressure had succeeded in thrusting my head out of the enclosure, it would be sustained until I am completely exposed. Strangely that has not happened. Instead, the momentum has all but evaporated.

*

I have been stuck in this position for what appears to be ages! I am in a kind of no-go situation. I am unable to push myself backwards; neither am I able to move forward. I am not feeling right. I am short of breath. I feel like passing out. Hey! Someone, please get me out, or else push me back to where I was comfortable!

*

Shh! I need to be silent and pay attention. For the first time I can hear what sounds like shouts of "press!", "press!!", "press!!!" The shouts are met with what appears to be groans of agony. Who then is the individual who judging from the groans appears to be in such pain? And who has the audacity to shout "press", "press" at someone who, judging from the groans, appears to be in such excruciating pain!

*

I might have nodded off for a short while—to be awakened by the resumption of the pressure I have been dealing with all along. It has all of sudden increased in intensity—to the extent of causing me to fear being crushed to death. My whole body is aching! I am not getting air; I am suffocating! I am being literally strangled to death! I can no longer bear this hellish situation. Whoever brought me to this precarious situation, please help bring it to an end: dead or alive! I can't take it any longer!

*

The same pattern continues to repeat itself! The sudden increase in the forces acting on me has been followed by an unexpected respite! Some time has elapsed; nothing new is happening, no going forward, no going backwards. I wish I could indeed do something to influence the situation, but I cannot!

The groaning has not only increased in intensity, it also appears to be drawing closer and closer to me.

The close proximity of the moaning leads me to think that perhaps I am stuck within the body of the person who appears without doubt to be experiencing a great deal of distress. Me stuck in the body of someone? I have for a while been aware of my situation, that I happen to be in an enclosed space surrounded by fluid. And it seems the enclosure happens to be within the body of an individual!

That is something I can hardly take in. If it turns out to be the case, how did I get there?

*

Despite the incessant shouts "press, press, press" nothing is happening to me. Indeed, there has been a pause in activities in and around me. I will take advantage of the calm to rest awhile.

*

Ach, that turned out to be short lived! Indeed, hardly had I closed my eyes in sleep than I was awakened by yet more cries of "Press, press, press"! The voice behind the latest order to "press, press, press" is different from all the previous ones. In fact, whereas the previous command sounded high-pitched, the one I just heard is deep-toned.

The intervention from the newcomer seems to have had the desired effect! Suddenly the pressure on me intensified, leading to my body being thrust a good distance forward. Now my neck and parts of the upper part of my chest have also emerged out of the tunnel.

The new development has been met with a great deal of excitement by those who seem to be behind the plot to evict me out of my rented accommodation, yes, my safe haven.

I can feel a strange hand, I better say a pair of hands, grasping me by the head and neck. Hey, what's happening? *Ouch*, unbelievable, but true, I am being *pulled* – or should I say extracted—out of the tunnel. *Hey, you*, don't you have any laws in your country? Indeed, is it a law-less society! You do whatever you wish with the body of an individual without first agreeing to their consent, right?

"Hey, please be careful you don't break my neck! My body parts are very fragile, don't you know!"

Ouch! That was a touch far from tender! My pleas indeed seem to have fallen on deaf ears! I may be wrong in my assertion—the impression I have so far of the individuals bent on evicting me from this safe habitation is that they are indeed bent on achieving their set goal without taking into consideration the trauma, indeed the discomfort being caused to me.

1B

AN INVOLUNTARY LEAP INTO TROPICAL HEAT!

At last, I have been completely expelled from my safe haven! The person from whose body I emerged is sitting on a wooden chair. She seems to be in agonizing, indeed excessive pain. I can see a good deal of red fluid oozing from her body; she appears so weak she seems unable even to breathe. I am really concerned for her wellbeing!

I am held tightly by someone. There is yet another person around. Despite the pain and distress the individual out of whose body I just emerged seems to be enduring, the two helpers seem to be ecstatic with joy!

I really find that strange. They should rather be doing what they can to ease the pain of the poor individual I just referred to rather than switching into a merry-making mode! Or is it because they are so used to the situation that they are hardened to the obvious suffering?

On my part I have not ceased screaming at the top of my voice since I left my safe enclosure. I am indeed inconsolable—for several reasons. In the first place as I indicated earlier on, I have been forced out from my accommodation without my consent. Secondly, the heat in this new environment is just unbearable to me!

Thirdly, the environment is just too strange for my liking. Above all, I am not able to bear the cacophony of noises pounding on my ears; they are just intolerable!

So I am really screaming—out of pain, fear, anger and frustration! "Someone put me back where I came from," I keep on yelling louder and louder. But no one seems to care. Or maybe they don't understand me?

Or is it because they are actually overjoyed by my arrival? Is it the first time they are witnessing the arrival of such a tiny being into their world?

That is really strange. Whereas I am still vehemently protesting having been expelled—without my consent, I must stress again—from the peaceful, serene environment of my previous habitation, those who apparently hatched the coup are clearly delighted, indeed ecstatically celebrating the arrival of a new member into their community.

No one seems to take my feelings into consideration. I thought again of the saying that it takes two to tango. How dare they make merry over my arrival into their midst when the agony I am going through should be obvious to them?

*

Despite the fact that I am still screaming, yes yelling at the top of my voice, I have managed to cast yet another quick glance in the direction of the individual from whose body I have just emerged.

She still appears to be in considerable pain. Even more worrying, she seems unable to sit, let alone to stand! The two women attending to her at least have taken note of the situation and have quickly spread a piece of cloth on the bare floor, and helped her onto it.

The floor of the enclosure where we are is not cemented, but rather covered with gravel. So only the thin cotton cloth is cushioning her body from the hard gravel!

Looking at her from this position, she appears lifeless! I am very sorry for her, for causing her such pain and distress—worse still, for endangering her life! I cannot imagine what she might have gone through during the whole time the ordeal lasted, especially during the whole time I got stuck in her body! Couldn't the two individuals who were clearly over the moon after pulling me out of her body have intervened earlier to end the stalemate? I am hoping and praying she manages to pull through this!

*

8

Ouch, I have just felt a sharp pain in the area of my belly button. That really hurt! My goodness, there seems to be no end to the ordeal I am subjected to. If that is the friendliest manner in which new arrivals are subjected to in this community, then I am in real trouble indeed.

I have just been wondering about the source of the pain I have just referred to. Hm! It has now dawned on me that I have lost direct connection with what was part of the wall of the enclosure I was resting in. Could the pain have been caused by the cutting of the cord that had been connecting me to the wall? So now I have no connection to the facility that has sustained me over the last several months! I am only wondering how I can survive in my new environment without my most reliable source of sustenance!

Where have I landed? In an oven? It is indeed very hot here. I feel like I am suffocating in the heat! Goodness me! I miss the cool environment I have over the last several months called home. Someone please get me out of here! Everything appears strange and weird indeed.

1C

MAMA'S HEARTY WELCOME

I don't know how long I have been screaming. My cries have been relentless, I must say—to the extent that the strange woman holding on to me appears to be at the end of her tether.

Fortunately for both of us, mother seems to have regained some strength. She has now managed to return to her seat.

"Please give me the little one; I want to have the first impression of him."

The lady taking care of me has done as requested and handed me to Mother. Though she appears to be in extreme pain, she has managed a broad smile. She is now cuddling me, drawing me close to her bosom. I am very sorry for her, but I cannot console her. She still seems to be in extreme agony.

*

After allowing Mother to hold on to me for a while, the same individual who placed me in her care —she appears to be in charge of everything going on here—has collected me from her and placed me in the charge of someone else. This new individual has been smiling at me ever since she took hold of me. I am not returning her friendly gesture though. Instead, I am still screaming at the top of my voice. The anger, yes, the fury of having been forced to leave the serene environment I have already referred to is overriding everything else.

The individual keeping me seems to be at a loss as to how to calm me down. "Calm down my dear one. Your mother is not feeling good. She is not in a position to take care of you, so bear with me."

I am not impressed—still yelling at the top of my voice. My voice is dwarfed by noises of various types—*maa, maa; baa, baa; meow, meow; hey, hey; cock-a-doodle-doo;* an intense ear-splitting, piercing, shrilling, barking, crowing. A real cacophony of noises—from humans and animals—two-legged and four-legged. Ach I can also hear honking and hooting in the distance!

Whoever brought me here, please help me out without delay! I surely did not bargain for this! The noise, the heat, the strange faces—they are too much for me; far too much for me!

1D

FIRST ENCOUNTER WITH TASTY BREAST MILK

I'm still in the custody of the stranger! She seems to be at the end of her tether from my relentless screaming!

Is it as a result of the screaming and yelling? I don't know for sure. What is beyond dispute is that I am feeling not only thirst but also hunger. How do I make my situation clear to these strangers? I do not understand their language, to me it sounds like Latin. So what is the way forward?

Well, I have decided on an additional tactic aside from the screaming and yelling—kicking my legs around and throwing my hands into the air!

"Don't worry my little one, I will take you to your mother. Hopefully she has regained enough strength to take care of you."

So the stranger is taking me back to the makeshift structure I referred to earlier on. Oh, look! Mother has emerged from the structure ahead of us. She is supported on each side by one of the two assistants who attended her. She can barely walk. She could best have benefited from lying on a bed; the attendants could then have wheeled her to her place of rest. Poor woman, she is biting her teeth together. I am still wondering why no one is giving her something to relieve her pain!

She is being led to a small building boasting two rooms which is about thirty metres away from the makeshift structure already referred to. The stranger bearing me has turned to follow her. Mother has now taken her seat on a wooden bed, in what is a really small room. It is quite hot inside.

The stranger has handed me to Mother. Though she seems to be in excruciating pain she seems to be more concerned for my welfare than that of her own. She has positioned me close to her left breast. She has pulled me even closer. Now she has placed her nipple in my mouth.

Something in me has urged me to suck on it!

Hey, this is really amazing, this is *really* amazing! Lo and behold the moment I began the sucking, all of a sudden, a cold, refreshing liquid began pouring into my mouth! This is really tasty, very well cooked, I should say. I would probably have added a bit more sugar, but never mind! Is it by sheer coincidence that it happened to be ready just at the very moment I needed it? Or was it especially pre-ordered for me?

It is the only pleasant experience to report about, out of a catalogue of mishaps and calamities I have been subjected to since the beginning of the events that culminated in my expulsion. I am still sucking on my mother's nipple—I want to fill my stomach to the last available space with this incredibly delicious milk. Ouch! I better not be taken away by greed and consume above what my tummy can take—otherwise I might see my belly bursting!

*

I might have fallen asleep, for now I am awakened. I am lying on the bed upon which mother sat whilst breast feeding me. She is nowhere to be found. I just wonder where she has gone! I am scared to be alone here. I have decided to scream out of fright.

Hardly had I begun screaming when a young lady entered the room. I am seeing her for the first time. I thought she was taking me straight to my mother—but no, she has taken her seat on a wooden chair. I am lying on her lap. She is smiling very warmly at me. Is that the culture of this new environment? Residents smiling at those they are not even familiar with. Indeed, why should she smile so warmly at me when she doesn't know me!?

I must indeed be ready for one surprise after the other! What surprise? Well, hardly had the strange woman taken her seat and placed me on her lap than she was surrounded by about half a dozen individuals

14

of all ages—both male and female. They all seem to have one thing in common—to have a look at the newest arrival in their midst.

Well, I have decided to pay them, as it were, in their own coin—by also staring at them.

"Hey, you, why are you gazing at me with such curious eyes! Haven't you seen anyone like me before?" I am asking them.

No reply! None of them seem to understand me! Instead, they keep on smiling, gesticulating and making some friendly gestures towards me!

1E

HELLO PAPA!

I might have fallen asleep again, for I am awakened by the sound of a group of humans entering the room.

I wish I could be allowed to rest undisturbed over a considerable length of time. Such an undisturbed rest period is what is needed to help me regain my strength following the arduous journey I have just put behind me. But no! There seems to be no end to the various sources of noise out there to disturb me. The group that has just entered the room is made up of an adult and four boys. They seem very elated—because of me? I don't know for sure.

"I am your Papa; these are your brothers—welcome home!"

"Welcome home." The four youngsters address me with one voice. I am really confused. I direct my gaze at the adult in the room.

"Papa? What do you mean by Papa?" I inquire.

The adult to whom my question is directed keeps on smiling instead of providing an answer. I am really beginning to think no one in the community I have met understands me! It is really strange—whereas I can understand them, they on their part seem unable to understand me! I only hope things will change with time. How can I communicate with them should this language barrier persist indefinitely?

This stranger who has introduced himself as my Papa seems to be in good spirits. He keeps smiling all the time.

"Welcome home, you are my boy number five!"

"Boy number five, really?"

"Of course, I am delighted to welcome you to my home. I have one wish though—do plead with whoever sent you to dispatch a girl next

17

time round. Your mother in particular will be delighted at that prospect. Indeed, she has always been yearning for a girl. So be the last boy, okay!"

"Be the last boy? I cannot make any sense of that! How can I have any influence on the type of babies who decide to visit them?"

"I will leave you with your brothers for now. Your Papa is a busy bee. He has to go and attend to other matters. I will see you later, my dear little boy!"

*

So I am now surrounded by four boys! Each of them is wearing a pair of khaki-coloured shorts. None of them is wearing anything above the shorts. I don't blame them for leaving their upper bodies bare, mind you. I will also not want to wear any tops in such hot weather. Is there nothing that can help cool things a bit? I do without exaggeration feel like suffocating in the sweltering heat! Maybe I should have chosen a different season in time when temperatures are mild for my journey—if indeed one can experience such a climate in my new home.

The biggest among the four lads surrounding me is addressing me.

"Welcome to our midst, my little brother. You have four big brothers. I am the eldest. I will introduce myself and leave the others to do likewise. My name is Kofi Ofosu, also known as Kofi Tano. I am called Kootano by all, which is short for Kofi Tano. I am 12-years old. Since I am the eldest of the group, you can also call me *Big Boss*. I will take good care of you. If any of these three lads try to be naughty to you, you report them to me, so I can teach them lessons in good manners and behaviour, okay? Now I hand you over to the next in line."

"Hi, little one. Here is your big brother Kwabena Osei, the next in line. Actually, according to Papa and Mama, a girl came before me. Sadly, she decided to return to where she came shortly after her arrival. I will take good care of you.

"By the way," Kwabena resumed after a short break. "Don't mind him," he pointed to his senior, "no one made him the *Big Boss* over anyone!"

"Don't listen to him," Kootano counters. "I am the eldest and so have the automatic right of leadership of the group. As far as that is concerned, it is beyond dispute."

"Being the eldest doesn't automatically make you the boss. I don't however want to argue the matter any further, so I am passing the baton to the next person."

"I am Kwaku Baafi, also known as Kwaku Amoah. I am five years old. I don't have anything to add."

"Hey, Kwame, it is your turn to introduce yourself," Kwaku urges the youngest of the group who appears shy and unwilling to open his mouth.

"Never mind," Kofi intervenes. "He is timid, doesn't want to talk. He is Kwame. He is two years old. Until your arrival he was the youngest. Now you have taken that role from him."

For a while there was silence in the room.

"Hey guys, come along, let's go and continue our game of football," Kwabena urges the others, bursting out of the room as he speaks.

"Yes indeed," Kofi and Kwaku shout in approval.

Soon all four of them, including timid-looking Kwame, are headed for the door.

"Hey little one," Kootano cries out, "take good care of yourself, we shall see you later. For now we are going out to enjoy a game of football!"

*

I thought I was the only guy at home; but no! Four big boys ahead of me! Having four big brothers is definitely a good thing. They will surely take good care of me. I can also learn from them.

The downside is that they may be tempted to adopt a patronizing attitude towards me. No; I will make it crystal clear to them at the very outset—no patronizing! They should also refrain from thinking because I am so small, they can bully me and order me around! No, I won't allow myself to be intimidated or coerced into doing anything that I do not approve of!

So now I know all the members of the family—Papa, Mama and the four big brothers.

*

Hey someone, please help cover the lower part of my body! I thought a towel or a piece of cloth would be wrapped tight around that part of my body. But no! The practice instead is for just a piece of towel to be laced across both legs. If for whatever reason I move my legs up and down, the towel is moved away, exposing my body in the process.

What is even more embarrassing—whenever I open my bowels, or my bladder, the whole world witnesses it! Don't I deserve some privacy? Of course, I do! I must without delay talk to Mama about this. Oh! It has just dawned on me once more that no one can understand me!

*

I can feel some pressure building up in the lower area of my tummy. Yes; I feel the urge to empty my bladder.

When I was resting in the serene enclosure I have been forcefully expelled from, I did not ask for anyone's permission to empty my bladder, so I just emptied it into the surroundings. What should I do now?

Hey someone, please, I want to empty my bladder; what should I do? They are just staring at me; no-one seems to understand me. No, I have to do something, before my bladder bursts!

Oh, this is embarrassing! I might have applied too much pressure on my bladder. It has unleashed a fountain of water splashing into the neighbourhood. The water from my body has drenched the clothes of some of the by-standers. Everyone has burst into laughter! I really thought the victims of the incident would be offended, yet everyone is clearly amused by it.

Well, it's not my fault. Remember, I just drew attention to my lower-body that needs to be covered. It wouldn't only prevent my exposure to the rest of the world, it would also prevent such incidents.

*

I am feeling yet another kind of pressure. This type of feeling is unfamiliar to me. I did not experience this kind of pressure in my previous home. This one is a pressure to open my bowels. I am trying to convey this to my mother, but my goodness, she doesn't get it! As I already indicated, whereas I am able to understand them, they don't seem to understand *me*. It is really strange. What should I do?

I have not been able to suppress the pressure to open my bowels any longer, so I have given way to it. My lower body is soiled; the scent is not pleasant. Hey someone, please come and clean me!

Oh! The same issue with the language barrier is back again. How can I communicate my urgent requirement to the rest of the present company? Once again, I am forced to resort to what to me is the only means at my disposal at communicating my needs to the rest of the world—howling and crying at the top of my voice!

This strategy as always bears immediate fruits—one of the strangers who is offering Mother a helping hand has arrived to take care of me. I find it very kind on their part to have taken the trouble to come over to offer Mother a helping hand; without doubt she will be very happy with any little assistance she can receive in these challenging times.

*

I have been picked up by yet another stranger, an elderly woman. She has ripped me completely naked! Exposing my nudity before a complete stranger—without my consent! Hey, what's going on here?!

I think she is just here to assist Mother—which is laudable. What I do not find quite proper though is that she failed to introduce herself to me. She should, to begin with, have smiled and said something like: "Hello my little one. I am Madam So-and-so. Don't be scared, I am not here to harm you—only to assist your mum. As a first step, I am going to give you a wash down." But instead of a gentle, courteous approach, she just grasps me and begins to undress me!

I have no idea what she is up to. I am watching attentively. She has placed me over her two outstretched legs. Holding me firmly with one hand, she has pulled a bucket filled with water closer to her, making use of her spare hand. She has now dipped a towel into the water in the bucket and is using the wet towel to rub my body. I find the water too warm for my liking. I would have preferred a cold shower in this hot climate. I am protesting, as usual by way of loud screams! The stranger appears unperturbed and dutifully keeps going about her task.

The rubbing with the towel has gone on for a while. Now I think she considers me clean enough! She has now taken hold of another towel, bigger than the first. Is she going to dip it into the water again? No, that is not the case. Instead, she is drying my body with the help of the dry towel.

I think she considers my body dry now, for she has put the dry towel away. I thought the ordeal was over, but no, that isn't the case. She has now picked up a small plastic container with a metal lid. She has opened the lid and is using part of the contents to cream my body.

Creaming over, she has taken hold of yet another small plastic container. She has opened the lid and gently sprinkled a white powdery stuff on the upper part of my body. Initially, I did not like the idea, but I have changed my mind because it has a really good smell! Is it a way of neutralizing the awful smell that hangs around my body after each bowel movement?

I really wish I could do everything on my own and that I do not have to depend on the goodwill of others to clean, wash and clothe me. Since that is not the case, I suppose I should be grateful to those helping mother rather than complain.

1F

MOSQUITOES BID ME A ROUGH WELCOME!

It has turned dark, very dark.

Hey sun, where are you? You just left without bidding me good-bye! That's not a courteous way of parting company with a new arrival in your realm of influence!

There is a positive side to the disappearance of the sun, though—it has driven away the crowd that poured into the house to bid me welcome. Now, at last, we are left on our own.

My four brothers have retired to bed in the other room. Yes, all four of them have to share one little room. I am yet to see the inside of it; whether they sleep on beds or on the floor, I have no idea. I hope I get the opportunity to satisfy my curiosity, indeed to find out for myself the state of affairs of that room. For now, I am left with Mama in our small room. I just wonder where Father has gone! I have no idea. In any case, it is night-time. I am spending my first night in this strange environment. I really do hope I can get a good night's rest—a proper peaceful rest.

There is a faint source of light in the room. I heard some members of the family refer to it as a Swiss kerosene lamp. The source of light is not strong enough to completely dissipate the darkness. Mother has just entered the room. I can only see her silhouetted against the light.

Mother is now lying beside me. I am lying between her and the wall. Mother is really thoughtful of my safety. Sandwiched. as it were. between her and the wall, there is no way I am going to fall onto the hard cement floor!

Poor me, despite Mother's presence, I am scared to death, so I have started crying. She pulls me closer to herself. I can feel the warmth of her body.

"Don't cry little one, I am here," she comforts me. That is really reassuring. Mother is very kind to me. I wish I was allowed to reside in her body indefinitely. I don't think it was her intention to expel me—it appears forces and powers beyond her control set everything in motion. Once initiated by external forces, my birth was inevitable and she lost control of events. Anyway, things have already happened. There is no point for me to spend all my time weeping over spilt milk.

For now, however, I will keep very close to her, because as it is, she is the only person I can rely on, not only for protection but also for her delicious breast milk. Oh, has it got anything to do with the fact that I just thought of breast milk? In any case, I am just beginning to experience hunger pangs!

Is Mama able to read my mind? Just as it dawns on me I am feeling hungry, she draws me even closer to her and places the nipple of her right breast in my mouth! It is perhaps superfluous to mention here that I have whole-heartedly seized on the opportunity!

I cannot stop repeating how tasty mother's breast milk is! How does she manage to cook such a delicious meal in her body? I can only wonder. Anyway, I am now filling my tummy with as much breast milk as I can lay hold on!

Hello! Who is causing this buzzing noise? Hey, whoever is the source of the disturbing noise, would you please shut up and give me some peace? But the annoying noise, instead of ceasing, persists. "Hey, whoever is disturbing my sleep, don't you have any sense of decency? Have you indeed lost all sense of civility and politeness for the new arrival in this strange environment?

"Ouch! That hurts!" That was a real sharp bite!

The awful creature that bit me is not only making a dreadful buzzing noise, but is determined to inflict injury—on such a little being like *me*! That is really outrageous.

Hey, Mama, please come to my rescue! Whatever is making this buzzing noise is determined to harm me. It's like the devil, the very epitome of all that is cruel and evil! Mama, please do something about it; please urge it to go away and allow me some rest.

Apart from her loud snores, no help seems to be coming from the side of Mother! She is lost in sleep. I don't blame her, considering the protracted labour and the subsequent stressful moments she has endured during the day.

Oh! Yet another vicious sting! There is more than one! This is more painful than the previous one. "Mama! Please rescue me from these horrible beings before it is too late!" Still no reaction from her! Well, I'll just have to resort to the last card in my armoury—screaming! —to awaken her, before these naughty beings cause me any further pain.

So I am yelling, very loud indeed!

"Shut up you little one and leave me in peace!"

Who was that shouting at me?! I have ceased crying in order to check what is going on. I have taken a close look at Mother. She is still deep in sleep. So it cannot be her shouting at me. Who then is behind the noise?

A short while has elapsed. I have resumed crying.

"Hey!" someone shouts, "Can you please shut up and leave every-one in peace!"

"Bang, bang, bang!" Someone is banging the wall separating the two rooms. Now I understand! My screaming is disturbing my brothers in the other room. Clearly, I'm disturbing their sleep—but their protests will not deter me from crying, even screaming louder. I am determined to persevere—until Mother wakes from sleep.

*

A sign of relief! Mother stirs—she's awake! Mother being awake doesn't seem to impress the beings assaulting me! One of them has just inflicted yet another sharp sting to the body: on my forehead, to be specific. Still yelling at the top of my voice I appeal to Mother with urgent eyes.

"Hey, dreadful mosquitoes," she says, "you leave my little one in peace!"

It is soothing, the realisation that Mother is awake. Better late than never! She will, no doubt, do all she can to protect me from these heartless aggressors. *Ouch*, yet another piercing bite! The offensive beings don't seem bothered by Mother's presence. On the contrary, they appear to become even more defiant!

"Hey you disrespectful and badly-behaved bunch of destructive insects, this is my final warning to you—to leave my little one in peace. Either you heed my warning or I will show you the red card!"

Did the mosquitoes understand the warning and decide to heed it? Or is it mere coincidence? Whatever the reason, they left me alone, enabling me to fall into a deep sleep.

1G

VISITORS UPON VISITORS

Day 2 of my arrival. Our home has become a centre of attraction. It all began moments after my arrival yesterday.

I thought today would be different—far from it, far from it! The day has hardly begun and yet I have already counted more than fifty visitors. I overheard a conversation between Kwabena and Kwaku on the same theme—namely the numbers pouring into our home. From the conversation I gathered that the settlement boasts around one hundred residents. If that is the case, it means about half of the population have visited so far.

There is indeed no end in sight concerning the coming and going. What I just cannot fathom is that some of the faces I am seeing today are among those I saw yesterday. And they are not only coming to greet Mother, they are also coming to stare at me! Is it not enough for them to have seen my face once!

I thought my arrival in my new environment is a private affair, a matter involving myself and other members of the nuclear family. That however does not seem to be the case. On the contrary, it appears to be a whole community affair. Indeed, everyone seems to be involved.

They all seem to be very excited; as if they are welcoming back home a family member who has returned from a long journey. Due to the almost unceasing comings and goings, I hardly get the needed quiet to rest; barely had I closed my eyes in sleep when I was awakened by the arrival of yet another stranger wishing to cast an eye on me!

*

A group of women accompanied by some little ones has arrived. It appears they have come with presents for Mother. Members of the community are not only flooding our home to congratulate Mama and have a look at me; they are also coming with gifts—in the main foodstuffs.

They carry the items packed in baskets and aluminium trays on their heads. My goodness, how do they manage to balance the loads on their heads? Not only the adults are carrying items on their heads, the young ones accompanying them are doing the same.

*

The community is not only showering her with various gifts—foodstuffs, firewood, buckets of water, etc.; some are helping in the performance of the daily chores of the home—cleaning, washing, cooking. I find it very kind of them, in view of the pain she without doubt appears to be enduring. How could she otherwise have mastered the challenges without their assistance?

*

Despite the help and solidarity they are offering, some of the visitors pouring into our home are too loud for my liking. Not only are they loud, I consider some of the words coming from the mouths of some of them as banter, mere banter! For example, one of them after staring at me for a while told me to my face: "You look so handsome, sweet baby. When you grow up, I will marry you!"

Marry me? What did she mean by that?

One of the visitors, a little girl, after looking at me closely, turned to a girl standing near her and began: "That little baby has a big head in comparison to his body size. I am told such babies grow up to become very intelligent!"

"Who told you so?" the other girl asked.

"One of my playmates!"

"I don't believe a word of it!"

"Why not?"

"My brother has an even bigger head. Take it from me—he is a good for nothing fellow!"

*

As I mentioned earlier, ever since my arrival there has been an unending stream of residents coming to have a look at me! If only the visitors would just take a look at me and leave me in peace. But no, almost every one of them wants to touch me, yes, wants to feel me! For the great majority of them just touching or feeling me does not seem enough—no, they also want to pick me up and hold me close, in some cases very close to their bosom! Why for God's sake do they want a close, indeed an intimate contact with me? I am just a new arrival in the community, a fellow resident. I am by no means their friend, let alone their bosom friend—so they better keep their distance.

I really thought Mother would make that clear to them, even draw the dividing line between me and these visitors. But no, she does not seem to be bothered. Apparently, it's a closely knit community, so no one raises an eyebrow on such matters. The problem seems to lie with myself. Is it me, I wonder, that needs to get used to the customs and practices of my new community?

*

I have had time to study the humans who have been pouring into our home. It appears there are two kinds of humans. Members of the first group are dressed like Mother—in delightfully coloured pieces of wax-print clothing. They have wrapped either one or two pieces of the wax print around their lower body. Some are wearing the same type of material as a blouse on the top. Others are wearing blouses made of other material or T-shirts as tops. Many of those so clothed have covered their heads with equally delightfully coloured headscarves. Some among the first group of visitors so described have little ones like myself fastened to their backs! Some of the little ones being carried in the manner just described seem not too comfortable with their situation and are yelling at the top of their voices. Will mother carry me around in such a manner

29

one day? The answer is not far-fetched, I think, for it seems to be a normal practice of the community.

Those in the second group of humans are easier to describe. Papa and my brothers belong to this category. Most of them are casually dressed in either a pair of trousers or a pair of shorts (boxer shorts). The large majority of the young ones are not wearing any tops. The bigger ones among them are either wearing casual shirts or T-shirts.

*

My goodness, there are so many new things unfolding before my eyes, I will require volumes to document everything.

1H

LOUD BEASTS DISTURBING MY SLEEP

I am retiring to bed for the second night. I hope I can have some peace-ful rest this time—not to be pestered by mosquitoes as was the case last night. I have in the meantime been breastfed by *lovely* Mother; my eyes have become heavy; so good night, everyone!

*

Hey! My joy of a peaceful night seems to have been premature, for the mosquitoes are back! Do I have to live with this nuisance the whole of my life? That is a really daunting prospect!

As if the annoying noise from the mosquitoes is not enough! I am also hearing what can only be described as a loud howling noise! It can be heard at regular intervals of about five minutes.

"Hey, you better keep quiet and give this new arrival some peace of mind to rest for the night!"

That might have worked—quiet has returned. But not for long, not for long! Yet another howling noise—this one quite close! I am really frightened.

"Mama, what is that?"

Silence!

Just as in the case of the previous night, she seems to be fast asleep again. I'm really frightened.

Yet another high-pitched howling! It appears to be drawing closer and closer. Is whoever or whatever is behind it aiming to attack us? I really wish I wouldn't have to wake Mother from sleep, but I am afraid,

I have to do just that! Yes, it is imperative that I draw her attention to the impending danger.

I have resorted to the same means available to me—yelling at the top of my voice. As in the case of the previous night, it has had the desired effect—mother is awake.

"Hey little one, what is wrong with you? Are you hungry? Have you soiled your clothes?"

Oh, yet another ear-splitting sound! Despite the fact that Mother is awake, it has been enough to increase my screaming.

"Hey, you silly owl, just keep silent and leave my little one in peace or I will show you the red card!"

Owl? What is an owl? I thought I only had the mosquitoes to contend with; but now the owl? What is it?

Yesterday the mosquitoes, tonight the owl! What else is there to disturb my nightly sleep?

Is it a way of calming me? Well, Mother has offered me breastmilk! I'm not really hungry, but, well, I cannot resist the temptation, so I'm sucking on her nipple right now.

*

I've been awakened from sleep by yet another loud noise! Unlike the one associated with the owl, this one seems to originate from very close—just behind our front door.

I was so frightened, I responded as usual with a scream.

"Ach! The little one is scared by the crow of the cockerel! Don't worry little one, they are not there to harm you. They are crowing to signify the beginning of a new day!"

Crowing to signify the beginning of a new day? I might have missed the sign last night. After the mosquitoes had kept me awake awhile, I might have plunged into such a deep sleep that I didn't notice the sound of the cockerel.

Back to the matter of the cockerel. Mother tells me their crow signals the beginning of the new day. What then will happen if they forget or refuse to send out the signal on a particular day? Will that mean we will have to remain in our beds the whole day?

Much of the things I am experiencing today are just similar to what happened yesterday, so I will spare myself the trouble of writing them down so as to avoid repetition.

11

THE TRIBE THAT MARKS ITSELF

Yet a new day. I am lying on Mother's lap. Father is here as well as a man who appears older than Papa. I am terrified by his looks. I am so frightened by his looks that I am screaming out of fright!

In reaction to my loud screams, the stranger has drawn back a bit. Mother has resorted to her usual strategy of trying to calm me down with an offer of breastmilk. I am enjoying it—tasty and soothing as usual!

The stranger has drawn closer; so also has Father. Father has grasped me by my two legs. Mother is holding my two hands.

What's going on? The stranger has come even closer; he has bent over me! He is holding a small object in his hands. He has drawn even closer to my body! Why has he come so near me? Mama, please push him away! *Ouch*, I can feel a sharp painful sensation to the right side of my face. I don't know how to describe it. It is a sharp, aching type of pain. I am screaming at the top of my voice! The evil-looking man might have inflicted a cut to my face because blood is flowing from my face. Part of my clothes is soiled in blood!

As if the pain he is causing me is not enough, he has rubbed some dark powered stuff into the cut! It is burning, a really excruciating pain. I am in agony—screaming at the top of my voice.

Mother as usual is trying to appease me with breastmilk. It has so far been her strategy. As in all previous cases, it seems to be working. Mother's milk—how strange! It seems to possess some magical powers—powers capable of numbing unpleasant sensations and situations, including pain, fear, distress, discomfort, etc.

I cast a glance at Papa and then to Mama. "Hey Mama, Hey Papa, why have you permitted this stranger to cause me such distress?"

No answer is forthcoming. Somehow, they appear to be unconcerned about my well-being.

Father has now turned to Mama. "That boy is certainly not amused by what is going on."

"Of course not. The problem is that he cannot understand us, so we cannot make it clear to him why he has to undergo the ordeal."

"Well, one day we will explain the matter to him—the fact that our Akan culture requires each one of us to keep our facial tribal marks, to help distinguish us from members of other population groups."

Being forced to undergo such pain just for the sake of keeping a mark on my face to distinguish me from others! My goodness, is there no other way of achieving that than by way of such a dreadful ordeal?

1J

DAILY RHYTHMIC SOUNDS

I have already made mention of the various kinds of noises that I am exposed to from various sources. One particular type of noise has become so regular, in the late afternoons usually, that I need to dwell on it a while.

I will do the best I can to describe it. I will start by dwelling on the nature of the sound. It can best be described as a regular, rhythmic *kum, kum, kum* sound. As I have in the meantime found out, the noise is associated with the pounding of fufu, a meal which is eaten every evening at home. From what I have so far gleaned from conversations of my brothers, it happens also to be the evening meal of almost every member of the community.

Even as I am compiling my report, the fufu meal for this evening is being pounded before my eyes. Kwaku as well as one of the strangers who have come to assist Mother are in the process of pounding. Each of the two is doing so with the help of a wooden pestle. They are standing facing a wooden mortar. A woman is sitting beside the mortar, facing both of them.

The woman sitting beside the mortar is placing one after the other chunks of cooked plantain and cassava into the mortar. Kwaku and the helper are pounding the chucks of plantain and cassava. The woman sitting beside the mortar is not only placing chunks upon chunks of the plantain and cassava into the mortar, but also ensures the crushed pieces of food do not fall from the mortar to the ground. I have observed the scene for a while. It appears there are no more chunks of food left to be pounded.

The task is not over though. Kwaku and the other person are still pounding the food in the mortar. The woman sitting near the mortar keeps turning the food while being pounded. From time to time she dips her hand into a bowl of water and smears some of the water around the food being pounded.

It is without doubt a laborious procedure. Both Kwaku and the other person seem to be sweating. Will I ever be called upon to perform such a laborious assignment? I can only hope that is not the case.

*

Mama has been served a portion of the fufu meal! I am on her lap right now. In one of the rare moments since my arrival in this community, I am settled and quiet—no irritation whatsoever. I am conversant with the fufu balls but not the soup. Yesterday the soup looked yellowish in colour. I learnt it was made with groundnut (peanut) butter. Today the soup to go with the fufu balls is red-coloured. They are speaking of palm nut soup. I understand it was obtained from the flesh of the palm nut fruit. Several fruits were boiled and then pounded in a special mortar for a while. The product obtained from pounding was dissolved in water. The mixture was then allowed to pass through a sieve. The solution was cooked with meat and/or fish for a while and then served with the fufu balls.

Everyone is urging Mother to drink as much of the palm nut soup as possible. My understanding is that palm nut soup as well as the soup made from peanut butter help in the production of breastmilk. Well, then Mama, do go ahead and drink as much of the palm soup as possible to ensure the continuous production of sweet and tasty breastmilk to feed me!

*

I find it really kind of the team of helpers who are helping Mother. Ach, they may think I am too young to count. Well, they are not aware I am able to do so. I have established that there are five to six of the helpers who have been around on every blessed day since my arrival. They are performing several functions—fetching water, sweeping the compound, cleaning the cooking utensils, washing dirty linen, preparing meals, and so on. I find it very kind of them, bless them.

*

Apologies but I have messed up my immediate surroundings with my excrement—again! It has soiled not only myself, but Mama as well. It is uncomfortable. I am screaming!

As I mentioned earlier, I think it would be advantageous if a towel, a piece of cloth or whatever, were to be wrapped firmly around my lower body to catch my excrement. Why that is not the case is beyond me. Is it perhaps because it will be uncomfortable to wear something of that nature in the hot weather? In any case, one of the helpers has quickly come over to help clean me. I am very grateful for the prompt attention.

*

I wish I could sleep through the night. But how can I do so when I do not possess my own room? Several matters distract me. Let me begin with myself. I just don't understand but I seem to get hungry quickly. It is Mother's custom to give me an abundance of milk to drink just before retiring to bed. At the end of that feeding session, I usually get the feeling it is enough to take me through the night.

But then, somehow along the way, I get hungry again, causing me to cry.

Next are factors, yes circumstances beyond my control that either keep me awake or awaken me from sleep. A couple of times during the night I feel the pressure to open my bowels or my bladder or both. Even when I consciously try to supress the urge, I am eventually overcome by the call of nature.

Then there are the mosquitoes that disturb me not only because of their buzzing noises, but because of their stingy bites! Oh, I nearly forgot to name another source of sleep disturbance—snoring itself! Whether from Papa or Mama, I cannot tell, but the fact is the loud nightly snoring I am exposed to does little to create an optimal bedroom environment for a good night's sleep!

1K

A ROLL CALL OF MY ANIMAL FRIENDS

I am now going to devote some time to the animals roaming freely in the compound. They too seem to have taken notice of the new arrival in their midst.

"How can you be certain?" someone might ask.

Well, as I rested on Mother's lap and enjoyed her breast milk, a couple of them, I guess a mother and her three little ones, headed towards us.

When they get very close, they stand still and direct their gaze at me. After keeping still for a while, all four of them cry as if with a single voice:

"*Maa, maa, maa!*"

On hearing this, Mother turns to them and remarks, "Hey, you, is that your way of bidding welcome to my little one?"

"*Maa, maa, maa!*" they cry again in unison!

After standing near me for a while, the gaze of each of them is directed at me as they stand there, before they turn to go away. As they go each one of them waves its tail in a distinctive manner. Is that perhaps their way of saying goodbye?

*

Initially I thought they were the only four-legged beings roaming the compound. But no, that is not the case. Indeed, I have identified a few other types—not only because of their features but also their distinctive cries.

41

I don't know their names yet; I will surely get to know them as time goes on. In the meantime I shall describe them on the basis of their distinctive sounds. I have just made mention of the type associated with "*maa, maa, maa*" cries. Next, I want to introduce the type which has the tendency to bark loudly the moment strangers arrive in our compound. There are two types.it seems.

There is another type of four-legged being which, whilst looking quite similar to those associated with the "*maa-maa-maa*" sounds, are a bit smaller in size. Though the sound emanating from them sounds a little similar to *maa, maa, maa*, on close attention it sounds more like *baa, baa, baa* than *maa, maa, maa*. So I will categorize this type as "*baa, baa, baa*"! Still on the subject of this group of four-legged beings, it may be premature on my part to draw conclusions.

Still, I get the impression that individuals of this group of four-legged beings are more hot-headed, audacious and uncultured than their bigger compatriots. Their manner is unruly, far from the calm, obedient and compliant attitude displayed by the *maa-maa* on their visit. This in any case is my subjective assessment of the matter—I may be wrong.

Next, I want to present a four-legged being that is far smaller in size than all the other three types already referred to. He–or is it a she? — appears to be a loner in the real sense of the word. Not only is it alone, it also seems to be very shy and reclusive. It singles itself out by dint of its distinctive "*meow, meow, meow*" cries.

Just by way of repetition—all the four different types of animals I have referred to are four-legged.

Finally, I want to present one type of animal yet to be mentioned. This type of animal is different from the others in the sense that it is endowed with two instead of four legs. Is it perhaps a way of compensating for the missing two legs? I have no idea. In any case this type of animal has something its four-legged counterparts lack—wings.

Yes, beside the two legs, they are endowed with a pair of wings with which they manage to fly short distances. I have so far identified only one type of their kind. They make various kinds of noises and sounds. The most notable is the loud noise which unsettled and awakened me from sleep on the very second night of my arrival in my new home. I have my own way of describing it—*ko-ku-koo-koo-ooo!*

I am yet to establish whether all the animals roaming in our compound belong to us. I am certain the two animals that keep on barking a good while of the time, especially the moment they spot strangers approaching our home, as well as *"meow the loner"* belong to us.

Why am I sure, someone may ask? The reason is that I see the same faces of the two sets of animals most of the time. Concerning the other types of animals, I keep on seeing many different types of them all the time.

Just as in the case of other homes of the settlement, our home is not demarcated with any type of wall. Put another way, our home is open to all—not just to the humans of the village, but also the animal population. Thus, during the day, animals from various parts of the community roam our compound in addition to ours. I guess the reverse is also true of our own animals.

Whether they are part of our own animal population, or from outside our home, the impression I have is that the animals roaming our compound have become so familiar with humans, that they seem no longer afraid of us.

1L

A CARING MOTHER AND HER MESSY BABIES

I mentioned earlier that I will document only incidents relating to the emptying of my bowels that can be described as beyond the ordinary. If the incident I am about to report does not qualify to be described as such, then what else can?

I was seated on Mama's lap not very long ago when I felt the urge to open my bowels. I realized it was an inopportune time—she was enjoying a fufu meal. Not wanting to disturb her meal, I did my best to suppress the natural call—to no avail! Aware of what Mama was engaged in at that moment, I tried to open my bowel gently, so she wouldn't realize what I was up to. Unfortunately, things did not go the way I had envisaged.

"Splash! Splash, splash"—a few ear-splitting sounds accompanied the watery stool rushing from me down below. The spillage from my bowels ended up soiling a good part of my immediate surroundings; some even ended up in the fufu meal mother was enjoying!

Initially, I thought she was going to dispose of the meal, but no, she did not! Instead she covered it, cleaned me up, and returned to enjoy her meal, as if nothing had happened!"

"Ugh; Mama! How can you continue eating that!" Kwaku wondered.

"Why not?"

"Ugh; that is disgusting! You saw with your own eyes what happened, didn't you?

"What?"

"Some of the shit ended up in the food!"

"And so what? I experienced an even worse incident in your case!"

"Really?"

"Yes; in your case, it involved an even bigger chunk!"

"Yucky! And you did not throw the whole thing away?"

"Throw away everything? No, I didn't. In the first place I did not have the time to cook yet another meal. Most importantly, it is regarded as a taboo in our culture to do so. It would imply me disowning you!"

1M

CALL ME BY MY CORRECT NAME

Day 7 since my arrival! There is unusual activity going on at home. Something special appears to be about to take place.

Kwaku, who appears as puzzled as I am, has turned to Papa.

"Papa, what is going on?"

"We are making preparations for the naming ceremony."

"Naming ceremony?"

"Yes, we are going to give your little brother a name."

"Did that happen in my case also?"

"Yes, every child gets a name when he or she is seven days old. That is what is going to happen to your brother."

"Am I allowed to watch it?"

"Only if you behave yourself and not turn unruly."

"I will try."

"It's not a matter of 'I will try' – you must be quiet if you want to witness it, okay?"

"Yes, Papa!"

*

I'm lying on Mother's lap. About half a dozen adults in addition to my parents have surrounded me. Father has started speaking:

"I am naming him after my maternal uncle, Nana Kofi Peprah. Indeed, without his kindness and generosity, I may not be alive today! At the time when my wife Amma was about five months pregnant with him, I was afflicted with a boil on my right thigh. In time it grew bigger

47

and bigger. For financial reasons, I was kept at home instead of being sent to hospital. Fortunately for me, Nana Kofi Peprah who lives several miles away happened to be here on a casual visit. When he saw my pathetic condition, he did not hesitate in arranging for me to be sent to hospital.

"'You have come just at the very last minute,' the doctor examining me told me 'Any further delay would have resulted in blood poisoning and your certain death.' So I am naming him Kofi Peprah, in honour of my kind-hearted uncle."

The speech is over. Mother has just handed me over to a stranger, who has taken a seat beside her. I am yelling very loud, not least because of the scary look of the stranger.

Mother and father are holding me, trying to calm me. There are two empty cups standing near the stranger. Father has poured part of the contents of a green-coloured bottle into one of the cups. Water has been poured into the second.

The stranger has picked up one of the cups. He has poured a few drops on my tongue.

"This is water." He has put the cup down. He now has the other cup in his hands.

He is now pouring a few drops of the contents on my tongue.

"This is alcohol!"

Alcohol?! I can feel a burning sensation on my tongue! My tongue is on fire! My screams have turned into yells, yells of agony and horror!

"Calm down, my dear, calm down, we are not going to harm you," Mother comforts me.

So the event is over. Thank goodness! I have survived, even though the burning sensation on my tongue has not gone away.

Is it a way of soothing me, of compensating me for the ordeal I have been made to go through?

"Stop crying and get something to drink, dear little one. You can drink as much as you wish!"

Oh, is it because of the burning caused by the awful-tasting liquid poured on my tongue? Indeed, for the first time ever, Mother's milk has lost its delicious taste! Is it going to be a temporary affair or is it going to persist? I really do hope it is not going to be permanent.

*

What a day, and what an experience! I have already spoken about the way babies are carried on the backs of some of the residents who came to have a look at me. I had reckoned with a day when it would be my turn to be piggy-backed. Well, the moment came sooner than I expected. Feeling somewhat bored lying on that hard surface of a mat that had been spread on the open compound beneath the shade of some of the trees growing in our compound, I began to cry.

"Kwame, go stand near him, to provide him with some reassurance," Mother said to Kwame.

"I am fed up with him!" Kwame replied sulkily. "He will never stop crying! You take care of him yourselves. It's your baby, not mine!"

"Hey boy, don't be cheeky!" Mother countered, attempting to give him a whack on the buttocks for his insolence. He appeared smarter than her though and managed to run away.

Next she vented her frustration on me: "You little one, stop screaming, everyone is busy here!"

But I wouldn't budge and kept screaming, now even louder and louder!

With desperation written in her face, Mother walked towards me, bent over my body, grasped me with both hands and pulled me against her body. I thought she was as usual going to give me breastmilk—but no! Still holding firmly to me, she bent slightly forward. Next she performed a series of manoeuvres which initially sent my heart racing out of sheer fright!

First she threw me literally into the air. Thinking I was going to land on the bare ground, my heart began to race within me! But lo and behold, I landed safely on her back!

For a short while I lay on her back, unsupported by anything! I was scared to the bones. For a while I thought I would lose my balance and fall to the bare ground! As I kept on crying, I instinctively held on tightly to her.

49

With me still lying unsupported on her back, she unfastened one of the two pieces of colourful wax prints wrapped around her body. In a manner which I cannot describe with words, she managed to wrap the cloth around her body in such a way that it enveloped me too. Initially my whole body, including my head, was covered.

I struggled for air—indeed for a while, I feared becoming suffocated. My fear was unfounded though. Mother hurriedly pulled the cloth away from my head, down to just below my neck. Next, she released both of my arms as well as my lower legs which had been covered. So here I am, securely fastened to the back of my dear mother! I am enjoying the warmth emanating from her body and the fresh air blowing in my face—the feeling is overwhelming.

Life on Mother's back! It has become a normal occurrence. Initially, I thought Mother would only occasionally fasten me to her back. Well, since I find it scary to be alone and my brothers are reluctant to keep what amounts to almost constant watch over me, Mother has been forced to carry me on her back most of the time that I am awake.

The implication is that I am usually fastened to her back as she goes about performing her daily chores—sweeping around the home, collecting water from the riverside, cooking meals, washing dirty clothes—the list of her household duties is endless.

*

From my observation so far, I have concluded that all my siblings who are boys constitute a disadvantage to our parents, in particular Mother. Whenever she carries me on her back around the community, I see girls who are about the age of Kwaku and Kwabena carrying babies on their backs! What even impresses me—the girls not only carry babies on their backs, some even manage at the same time to play community games like 'ampe', a game which requires the player to jump and throw one leg into the air while balancing on a single one! It is astonishing how they manage to do this with babies fastened to their backs! For reasons that I cannot explain, it appears boys are not endowed with similar abilities.

*

"Meow, meow, meow!"

Ouch! My good friend has made a stop near me—I am lying on a mat spread in the open, near the kitchen.

"Meow, meow…" I have returned the greeting. From the expression on its face, it doesn't appear to have understood me.

There is silence. He doesn't seem to want to speak to me! Ach, that is not fair on your part! I am just returning your greetings, and you don't seem to bother. Or didn't I imitate you perfectly enough?

I will try again. *Meow, meow*; hey good friend, is that okay?

Ach, it looks so sad, it appears it is sad, hungry, perhaps.

"Wait, my good friend. I will ask Mother to give you some of the milk intended for me, okay!"

Ah, it seems unimpressed with the idea that it has started moving away.

"Hey, you, just wait a moment!"

Ach, it seems to have made up its mind, for it has moved on. I really want to be friends with it. I want it to become my playmate.

*

Madam Work-Alcoholic! I have on not a few occasions reported about the daily tedious chores Mother has to accomplish. Today was no exception—it involved hewing wood for use at home. Firewood plays a key role at home. No cooking can be done at home without firewood. From my observation so far, it appears to be the only source of heat for cooking not only at home, but everywhere else in our settlement.

I heard Mother say that she built up a stock prior to my birth. Other members of the community also presented her with some after my birth. Well, we have in the meantime exhausted our stock, hence the need to replenish it.

Before collecting wood, she gave me some milk to drink and then placed me in the care of Kwaku. She then went about the tedious task of hewing the wood with the help of an axe. After a while she managed to hew a large pile of firewood.

"Everyone, get ready. We will soon be on our way!" she announced. She assigned loads to my two brothers based on their abilities. She left the best part of the load for herself.

*

Today's entry is about our home. I have now been here for a couple of weeks, so I have a fairly good picture of what our home looks like. It is made up of a small rectangular mud building measuring about ten metres in length, five metres in breadth and three metres in height. It is roofed with corrugated aluminium sheets.

The building has two rooms. I share one room with my parents; my brothers occupy the second. About thirty metres away from the main building, towards the bush that borders our compound, is a smaller building, about a third of the size of the main building. It is the kitchen. It also serves as the storage for foodstuffs, firewood and other utensils such as wooden mortar for pounding fufu.

In one corner of the kitchen is a makeshift stove built of clay. It has been constructed in such a way as to permit cooking two items at the same time. There is another stove on the open compound between the two buildings. From my observation so far, much of the cooking, as well as the day-to-day activities of the family, take place in the open space between the two buildings. Indeed, apart from rainy days, most of the cooking is done in the open. On rainy days and also when we retire to bed, the outside stove is covered with a sheet woven from palm branches to shield it from the rain.

Near the open stove just referred to is a small wooden structure— the chicken coop or hen house. Ah! Our chickens! They rarely spend time in the house built for them. I am not claiming to be able to read their minds, but I guess they may be saying to each other: "Why spend our day in this cage and die of boredom, instead of mingling with the humans so as to enjoy their action-packed lifestyle, indeed a life full of adventure and activity?"

Indeed, my observation is that they have become part and parcel of the human community here. Familiarity, it is said, breeds contempt! Indeed, the animals at our home, the birds included, have become so used to the humans they fear us less. On many occasions they have just snatched food from the hands of the human beings, in some cases just at the time when they are about to put it into their mouths!

*

There are several trees growing in the compound of the home. Some bear fruit. I observe my brothers climbing the trees from time to time to pick some of the fruit. I hear them calling the fruit names like mango, orange, coconut, etc.

Oh, I nearly left out the rectangular structure where I first emerged from Mother's body! It is about ten metres away from the kitchen towards the bush which borders on our home. Apart from rainy days when the family seek shelter in the buildings referred to, most of the activities of the day are conducted in the open.

Concerning myself, I spend most of the daytime either on the back of Mother or on a mat spread on the hard floor beneath a few orange and coconut trees growing just near the kitchen building I referred to earlier. The trees provide shade from the sun. I really prefer this arrangement to sleeping in the room during the day—the rooms turn really hot during the day.

If I am quiet and settled, I am allowed to rest in peace. If, for whatever reason, I become unsettled and begin to cry, initially Mother dispatches one of my brothers to check on me. Usually, they stand beside me for a while as a way of reassuring me. If despite such a step I continue to cry, Mother comes to pick me up and breastfeeds me. If in the process I fall asleep, she returns me to my original position.

On a fairly regular basis some of the domesticated animals roaming the compound draw quite close to me whilst I am lying in the open. Is it out of curiosity or perhaps a way of saying hello? I thought the behaviour of the animals would cause a stir among the family, in particular Mother. But no! The rest of the family seem to have developed such trust in our four- and two-legged compatriots that none of them seem to entertain the slightest fear of the beings ever doing anything to harm me.

*

I wish indeed I had my own room where I could be placed as needed to enjoy some rest, away from the persistent noise and hullabaloo of our home. Dream on! That would indeed involve my parents having to erect a house boasting at least six rooms, so each of us could lay claim to one! Ouch! I better say at least eight rooms, for from what I am hearing my parents, Mother in particular, will not entertain the idea of stopping to give birth to more children until they are blessed with at least one girl. As things stand, I will have to share my room with Mother for a while.

*

Hey there, don't you have anything for me to play with? I am just lying on my back on this hard surface—with nothing to occupy me. If you don't have any game for me then send me my four-legged friend. I don't mean the one associated with the *baa, baa* sound. They are not only loud, but quite stubborn. No, I prefer the little fellow; the one that goes about making *meow* sounds. I really enjoy his company, very soothing.

*

Mother, the busy bee! I really wonder how she is able to cope; where she gets her energy from! She is indeed on her feet from the rising of the sun to its setting every day of the week!

Indeed, she is on her feet from the rising of the sun to its setting—every day of the week! The first thing she does on waking up on a typical day is to sweep around the compound using a broom. Next, she washes the dishes left over from the previous evening's meals. She usually sends Kwaku and Kwabena to the Nwi River. There are times though when after sweeping around the compound and washing the dishes, she also heads for the Nwi River to fetch water for the household.

Poor me, I wish I could leave her in peace to go about her chores. I don't know how to put it. Though I consider the right thing to do is to leave her in peace, that is hardly the case. Anything that sets in to make me uncomfortable, like hunger, thirst, the soiling of my body, or just being scared of being left alone usually triggers a reaction within me which ultimately leads to me screaming and yelling at the top of my voice—which in turn forces her to have a look at me and eventually fasten me to her back. Imagine having to perform such a busy schedule with a baby stuck on your back!

After performing her basic morning chores, she prepares breakfast for the family. Thereafter, she gets ready to join Father on the farm. Sometimes she carries some of the breakfast along for Father. What she usually does is to take the cooking utensils and the uncooked food along—to be cooked on the farm.

*

There was drama, pure drama at home today. Throughout the day, I felt unwell. I lost my appetite and very reluctantly accepted milk. As expected, my parents became very concerned. In the course of the day my body began to turn hotter and hotter.

Then all of a sudden my whole body became stiff. This was followed by incessant shaking and jerking of my legs and hands. Everything happened so suddenly! Mother was keeping me on her lap and lost control of me. Moments later—bump! I fell to the ground! That's all I can remember!

For a while thereafter it felt like I was no longer in my body. Instead, it appeared to me as if I was walking in a beautiful rose garden. I felt peace and tranquillity—nothing comparable with the heat, the cacophony of noise and the stress I have been exposed to since I was forcefully evicted from the tranquil enclosure in Mother's body several weeks before.

As I was enjoying the calm and peaceful surroundings, suddenly I was transported from the tranquil setting. For a while it felt as if I was just swimming in empty space. Then suddenly, the scene changed, and to my utter dismay, I realized I was back in the familiar environs of my earthly home.

If I was upset and angry on the realization I was back home, what really alarmed me as I was coming back to myself was the realisation that I was completely soaked through with cold water! I did not need to guess where the water came from, for I realised I was surrounded by about half a dozen individuals, familiar and unfamiliar faces, all of whom were actively pouring cold water on me by means of various containers and vessels in their hands.

"Hey, what's going on here?!" I screamed aloud. "For heaven's sake, please stop pouring water on me!" And I yelled even louder. To my surprise, the moment those surrounding me heard my scream, they began shouting and clapping their hands in absolute delight!

"Thank God, he is back to life!" I heard someone exclaim.

"Yes indeed; I am absolutely thrilled!" Papa shouted, hopping around like a little child as he spoke. "Words cannot express how delighted I am. I am indeed over the moon!"

The jubilation went on for a while. As it did, I kept on wondering what all the fuss was about. I thought it was me alone who could not make sense of what had just transpired at home. Well, I was wrong, judging from the conversation that ensued shortly after Mama had dried me, changed my clothes and placed me on her lap and began breastfeeding me.

"Mama, why did we have to pour water on Kofi?" Kwame inquired.

"He experienced a 'sky possession!'" she said.

"Sky possession?" Kwabena said, surprise written on his face.

"Yes, that is what it is. When children experience 'sky possession', the only thing that helps is to quickly pour cold water on them. Time is of the essence. Failure to act quickly could result in them being taken away."

"Taken away? Where to?" Kwame wondered.

"Into the spirit world; far beyond the skies!"

"Into the spirit world? Is that really true, Mama?" Kwame was really puzzled.

"Yes of course!"

"I cannot believe such a fairy tale!" Kwabena laughed.

"Hey, Kwabena, how dare you challenge your mother?"

"What you are saying is based on superstition. One of my friends whose brother experienced something similar, brought the matter up in class. Our teacher told us the condition is known as febrile convulsions."

"Fiba Kovu....kovu?"

"No Mama! I said febrile convulsions. You say it after me."

"Fiii—fiii…"

"No, no, I meant febrile convulsion!!" That is typical Mama—always struggling to pronounce anything that is not Twi!

A short silence followed, broken by Kwabena.

"Mama, do you want to try again?"

"No, I won't—I don't want you kids to make fun of me."

"Well, if you don't want to learn, leave it. In any case Kofi's problem was not due to any spirits from the sky coming to steal him from us! We learnt at school that it happens when the body temperature rises above a certain level. Several conditions can lead to the rise of the bodily temperature. In this particular case, I guess the likely cause is malaria. Our teacher told us that what needs to be done in such a situation is to take immediate steps to bring the temperature down. That is what happened when we poured the cold water on him. The reduction in the temperature caused Kofi to recover. Do you understand now, my dear Mother?"

"No, I don't. You children of this age think you know better than we of the old generation! What happened had nothing to do with a rise in temperature caused by malaria. No, it was the work of evil spirits that attempted to snatch him from us. The cold water helped drive them away!"

"I can never believe that!"

"Hey, you impudent one, leave me in peace to breastfeed my little sweet prince!"

So peace returned.

I am not interested in the argument. What is important to me is that I have recovered. It was really scary though—not only because of the strange experience, but also because of the cold water poured incessantly on me—for a while I thought I would drown in it!

*

I am feeling a bit feverish. I only pray I do not experience yet another episode of 'sky possession'. But the febrile convulsions are becoming quite frequent occurrences! The forebodings that precede them are now becoming familiar to me. They usually begin with a feeling of heat in my body. Though Mama has no means of measuring my temperature, she usually notices the change quickly—using the back of her hand to feel my body when she fastens me to her back. On one occasion I felt so hot that she later told Father it felt as if her back was on fire! If they act quickly enough, they sometimes manage to prevent matters escalating into seizures.

Today, the remedy they tried on me was administered by way of an enema. That is one of several avenues of dispersing the complaint, I should add. Sometimes the same herbal formula is administered as liquid by mouth or as a suppository or a cream. Oh, I nearly left out the drops! The drops on their part may be applied to the eyes, the ears or the nose!

Sometimes my condition improves after undergoing treatment. On other occasions, the measures do not lead to a cure. Indeed, there have been instances when I have experienced the 'sky attacks' even as I was undergoing herbal treatment.

Today, after recovering from yet another 'sky attack' in as many days, Father consulted the help of yet another traditional healer. Moments later Father returned accompanied by the medicine man. With Mama holding firmly to my body, the strange man poured libation on the ground close to my legs, in the process invoking the assistance of the gods to protect me from the spirits of the sky. Finally, he fastened a talisman to the end of a brown thread and hung it around my neck.

"That will help repel the spirits responsible for the 'sky possession'," he reassured my parents.

I will wait and see whether the amulet can deliver what its owner has promised.

1N

A WEEK IN THE LIFE OF A PEASANT FARMER'S BABY

I just don't know what's going on. Mother seems to be getting ready for something. She has fastened me to her back. Next, she has placed several items—a few cooking utensils, vegetables, salt, cooking oil, etc.—on an aluminium tray.

Now she has turned to my brothers.

"Get ready boys; we are heading for the farm to fetch some food-stuffs. Our supply is running low!"

"Mama, you better stay away from the farm. You delivered a baby not long ago. It is too early to strain yourself!" That was Kwaku playing the big adviser. Is he doing so with his own interest in mind, well aware he will have to accompany Mother to the farm?

"Well, you are right," Mother replies. "I have no choice though; we are running low on our stock of foodstuffs."

"Can't you get someone to harvest for us?"

"Who?"

"Someone!"

"Well, I have no one in mind. Over the last several days we enjoyed the kindness and the solidarity of other members of the community. Well, there is a limit to what they can do. They also have to go about their own busy schedules—like anyone else in this farming community."

"Who will take care of the little one?" Kwaku inquires, pointing at me.

"I will take him with me."

"Take that little one to the farm? You can't be serious!"

"I *am* serious."

"How will you carry him there?"

"I will fasten him to my back, how else?"

"That little baby?"

"Yes of course. I did the same thing with you when you were just like him!"

"Gosh, I don't remember!"

"Well, now, you know!"

*

So the poor peasant baby that I am is being initiated into the daily routine of my parents' trade! From what I have gleaned from the conversation that has gone on between Mama and my big brothers, Father has already left for the field. He is said to have left early at dawn to perform various duties ahead of his actual daily work schedule on the farm.

Among others, I hear he will first go round to inspect traps he has laid in the forest with the aim of catching various animals roaming in the woods. Laying traps to kill other beings? That doesn't sound very friendly of him! Well, perhaps I am too young to understand! I will definitely query him on the matter one day.

After inspecting his traps, he will spend time tapping palm wine. From what I gathered from the conversations already referred to, wine can be obtained from tapping the palm tree. Money obtained from selling the wine helps support the family, I am told.

After he has executed those early morning chores, he is expected to continue the task of preparing a piece of land for planting food crops that will sustain the family in coming years. Concerning Mother, my understanding is that on reaching the farm she will cook lunch for Father after which she will perform various chores including harvesting foodstuffs to replenish dwindling stocks. I am just wondering how she can manage to cook food on the farm. Well, I will allow myself to be surprised!

So we are all set to leave home for our walk to the farm and I am stuck to the back of Mother!

I must mention that just prior to fastening me on her back, she gave me ample time to fill my belly with milk. "Drink as much as you can, my little one; you will not have the opportunity to do so whilst we are on our way!" For certain, Mother couldn't imagine I understood her advice. But I did! So, I did as instructed and drank as much of the tasty milk as there was space in my little tummy to accept.

As I did so Kwame came close and cast an envious look in my direction. Oh, poor him! He does not seem to have come to terms with the fact that he is no longer allowed the privilege of enjoying delicious mother's milk! Of course, he and Kwaku were well cared for—Mother cooked a breakfast of boiled plantain and kotomire sauce for them—*ampesi*, as they refer to the meal. Strangely, mother did not take part in the meal. When asked why by Kwaku, she replied that her stomach "has still not awakened from sleep!"

That is really strange to my ears! She is already up and going and her stomach is still asleep? Really bizarre!

*

We are now on our way to the farm. As already stated, I am fastened to Mama's back. Kwaku is leading the way; Kwame is following close ahead of Mama. Oh, and I nearly forgot to mention it—our two dogs are accompanying us. Why are we leaving the cat and the other animals behind? I have no idea.

Someone may ask me: where are your two other brothers, Kofi Fosu and Kwabena Sei? From what I have so far gleaned from the conversations that have been going on since I joined the "team" Kofi Fosu, my oldest brother, is undertaking an apprenticeship in a tailor's shop at Akuase, a town about seven miles to the north of our little village. He comes home only sporadically.

Kwabena on his part is attending school at Afosu, a town which happens to be about four miles to the south. There is no school in this little village. A relation of Father's—bless him—has opened his home to him to enable him to attend the local school. He comes home during the school vacations.

Our home happens to be the first building on the left side of the road when someone approaches the little settlement from the north. It appears our farm is located to the south of the village. So we are walking through the entire length of the village.

It is a small settlement so we can walk through it in no time at all—but for the fact that Mother keeps stopping at short distances along the way to greet virtually everyone who comes our way. The fellow residents on their part seem to be interested in only one thing—to cast a look at the little one fastened to her back!

The ritual is almost the same—first Mother stopping to exchange greetings; next, they move to her side to have a close look at me. If only they would be satisfied with a quick look at me! But no, without exception, they all have to take hold of my little hand and shake it—and not always gently, I should say. Indeed, some shake it vigorously, as they would do in the case of an adult!

Next follows the comment that has become familiar to my ears: "Boy, you look so handsome!" Why don't they leave me in peace? Frankly, I'm becoming fed up with them!

At last we have reached the outskirts of the village. I thought by now we would have left the lorry road and been walking along a bush path; but no, we are still walking on the road. I am scared to death—imagine a vehicle passing by at top speed and the driver unable to bring the vehicle to a halt before reaching us!

*

Well, what I have feared has come to pass; a vehicle has just passed by, coming from the direction we are heading for. It has now become clear to me why Mother has no concern about walking on the lorry road. The surface of the road is not smooth; indeed, there are several potholes in the road, so the vehicles travelling along it are forced to slow down and travel at a slow pace.

The vehicle that just passed was indeed travelling at a snail's pace. Besides being overloaded with humans and goods, a fact that slowed its progress, the driver had to swerve the vehicle from time to time to avoid the numerous potholes, further slowing the pace at which it could travel. The fact that it was traveling at such a slow pace led me to ask myself—wouldn't it have been better for the passengers to walk to their destinations rather than subject themselves to such an ordeal?

It is superfluous to mention here that Mother had all the time in the world to direct Kwame and Kwaku to a safe position along the edge of the road before doing the same herself. The vehicle has in the meantime disappeared from sight, along a bend in the road. It has indeed disappeared, though not the trail of dust it has left behind. My goodness, I am becoming short of breath. I can only hope the dust does not completely clog my delicate lungs and force them to shut down. Hopefully that is the one and only vehicle we will encounter on our way.

*

Oh! I thought I had dealt with the only source of annoyance. Well, my joy has turned out to be premature, for here comes yet another menace—a housefly! *Ouch*, it has made a stop on my forehead! I am terrified! I am shouting at the top of my voice.

"Kwaku hurry up!" Mother shouts. "Get behind me and check on your brother."

My dutiful brother has done as instructed.

"I cannot find anything wrong with him!" he proclaims, after casting just a casual glance in my direction.

"Hey my friend, are you blind? Have a closer look!" I am yelling at him! If only he can understand!

Mother is clearly unconvinced by Kwaku's report for she has loosened the cloth fastening me to her back and pulled me to herself to have a look herself. The troublesome fly, sensing danger, has hastily vacated its position on my face and flown away.

Having convinced herself everything is okay with me, Mother returns me to my previous position.

After walking on the lorry road for a while, we left it and joined a footpath leading directly from the road and heading into the woods. The footpath is narrow. It is being encroached by thick bushes growing on each side, rendering it almost impassable.

"Mama, why has the path been left in such a poor state? I am scared to walk on it for fear snakes could be hiding in the bush." Kwame is the first to complain.

"Don't scare me with talk of snakes hiding along the path!" Mother scolds him. "If you are not happy with the state of affairs, the right person to lodge your complaints with is your father. He and the other men using the path should arrange to clear the path of the encroaching bush on a regular basis."

Kwame appears to be satisfied with the response, for he has kept quiet.

We are making progress. Initially, I was not keen at the idea of Mother taking me to the woods at such a tender age. Nevertheless, I am enjoying the experience. Oh, what is that? I can see a couple of flying creatures. They look similar to our domesticated birds, the only difference being they are far smaller compared to our birds. Oh! how lovely, the sweet melodies emanating from their beaks! *Hey!* I have spotted two little beings hopping in the branches of a tree we are just passing.

"Look at that pair of squirrels!" Kwame exclaims, having just spotted them.

"What a pity!" Kwaku exclaims and brags: "I left my catapult at home. I would have killed both with a single stone and invited everyone to a feast of roasted squirrel meat!"

"How can you kill two squirrels with a single stone?" Kwame wonders.

"That is typical of Kwaku blowing matters out of proportion!" Mother says.

"I am not exaggerating! You just wait and see! Next time I will bring my catapult along and put my words into action."

"Well, for now let's concentrate on our walk."

"Okey dokey!"

It appears to be quite a long walk. We have in the meantime left the thick vegetation behind us. It has given way to what appears to be a cocoa farm which does not seem to stretch very far.

*

Mother asks everyone to stop. "We have arrived," she says.

"Really? But we have not been here before?"

"Yes indeed. This is a virgin forest. Father is clearing it for cultivation. It will provide us with food, not this year, but the next."

Oh, I can see Father! He is heading towards us, a broad smile on his face. He has a machete in his hands. He is sweating profusely. I wonder what he has been up to.

He has turned to address Mother: "It has been a busy day so far; first I inspected the traps; no luck. Next, I tapped the palm wine. I got here about an hour ago; I have so far managed to clear an area covering about five square meters."

"Well done, my dear!"

He has now directed his attention to me! "Welcome to the farm, my little one. I am in the process of clearing the thick forest undergrowth, getting it in good shape for the cultivation of foodstuffs. It is a tough, bone-breaking job. That is men's work; that is exactly what you will be doing one day!"

"That is what I will be engaged in when I grow up! That is disheartening, really disheartening! Where will I find the energy to perform what, without doubt, appears to be a really tedious undertaking! What a prospect! Can you please take me back where you collected me from?"

He is gesticulating in a manner that leads me to believe he did not get what I said. I should not have made the comment in the first place, well aware no one here understands me. Never mind.

Oh, I can see two gentlemen at work on the field. They look younger than Papa. Why are they working in our field? Kwaku has turned to Papa. "Papa, why are those two men working in our field?" He has asked Papa the question that has just crossed my mind—could he have read my mind?

"They are my day labourers."

"What is a day labourer?"

"I employ them on a daily basis to help me clear the field. It is too much work for one person."

"Do you want to engage me also as a day labourer?"

"Well, my little one, I will be happy for any assistance I can get. You are too young for the job though."

"No, I am not!"

"Okay then, next time I will find you a small machete so you can join us!"

"Mark my words," Mama says, shaking her head. "Children who create the impression of being eager to help their parents when young end up as lazy-bones when they grow up!"

"Hey, Amma, where did you hear that?"

"From my late father!"

"I don't make much out of it."

"Why not?"

"Do you want me to believe every wild assumption, conjecture, hypothesis, etc.?"

"This is not an assumption; it is an established fact!"

"Well, I don't want to prolong the matter. Let us concentrate on '*the now*,' how I can get the job of clearing the land for cultivation done!"

"Yes, my Lord."

"I am not your Lord, I am your husband."

"Yes, my dear!"

"Whatever!"

I am really enjoying the time. It is a welcome change. With no toys to play with, life at home can be boring.

Mama has turned to Papa again: "I will breastfeed the little one to help get him to sleep. Hopefully that happens quickly. I will then prepare a makeshift sleeping place out of broad leaves of a banana or plantain plant. I will then leave him in the care of the two boys. Finally, I will hurry to harvest foodstuffs from one of our adjacent crop farms and prepare lunch for everyone."

"Go ahead, my dear, and do as you deem fit. I will return to carry on with my assignment."

*

66

I might have fallen asleep, but am now awake. Mother has finished preparing the meal—boiled plantains and yams plus boiled and grounded green kontomire leaves laced with palm oil. The smell of the sauce is mesmerizing. I wish I were big enough to enjoy it! As it is, I have to wait for quite a while.

Everyone seems to be enjoying the meals. Ouch, the two casual labourers appear to be really hungry! The rate at which they are gulping down the food, I doubt there will be enough for the rest of us. Poor Kwaku and Kwame lost in the competition. I think Mother should have served each one separately. Ach, I forget, there are not enough plates even at home to go around for everyone, let alone here on the farm.

*

Mother has ended her day's activities on the field. She is preparing to leave for home. I am fastened to her back. She has packed items into two woven baskets. The big one contains three hands of plantain and a few tubers of yam. It is meant for Kwaku. The smaller basket contains a hand of plantain, meant for Kwame—loads are distributed in line with the motto 'each according to their abilities', I guess.

Mother's load is unusually heavy—beyond anything that I can imagine!

I heard her telling my brothers that there is a festival coming up next week. During the festive period, which will last three days, residents are forbidden to work on their fields. There is thus the need for her to carry home a more than the usual supply of foodstuffs—cassava, cocoyam, plantains. It is a real heap of foodstuffs that has been harvested. I ask myself, how does she get everything home?

From my own reasoning, the more convenient way to go about the matter is for her to carry part of the load home today and return to pick up the rest tomorrow. That doesn't seem to be what she has in mind. Judging from her actions, she is trying to pack the entire haul onto an aluminium tray she uses to carry loads home. Mother is really skilled in her trade.

Contrary to my thinking, she has managed to pack the entire pile onto the single tray. How did she do that? The answer is that she used what I will call a layer-by-layer strategy. She begins by skilfully arranging the foodstuffs into a circular layer on the round-shaped aluminium tray. Next, she builds a similar layer on top of the first. So on and on she keeps creating the layers, one layer on top of the other. In the end she ended up with five layers!

The question now is—how can she manage to lift the heavy load from the ground onto her head? And if she somehow manages to get the load onto her head, how will she manage to bear the heavy load on her head and at the same time carry me on her back and walk the distance home!

"Koo Gyamfi, come and assist me lift the load from the ground!" she calls out to Father. He is still at work, the other busy bee of the family—busily clearing the weeds that are encroaching on the young cocoa trees and preventing them from flourishing.

Father has responded to the call and has arrived at the scene.

"Hey, are you sure you can manage that, my dear?" is his first question

"Please get the load on my head and leave the rest to me."

"Well, I'm aware I married a *Power Woman*, yet this one is without doubt clearly beyond the ordinary, even in your case."

"I asked you to help me get the items onto my head and not to run a commentary on my abilities!"

"Okay, I'm keeping my mouth shut!"

*

Well with Father's help the tray packed with items to the high heavens is now on Mother's head. So, we are on our way home, Kwame and Kwaku in front, Mother following them, myself fastened to her back.

Father has gone back to continue work on the field being prepared for cultivation.

He told us he intended to work a few more hours before returning home.

So, I am fastened to the back of Mother. The items she is carrying on her head are literally reaching to the high heavens. It is really scary. I just hope and pray she experiences no mishaps, for example stepping into a pothole, which could dislodge some of the items and cause them to land on my delicate head!

*

Fortunately, Mother has made it safely home. How does she now get the load on her head safely to the ground? "Someone, hurry up, run to one of the neighbouring homes and ask whoever is around to come over and help me get the load safely to the ground!"

Kwaku runs to look for assistance as instructed. A little while elapses and mother is really sweating under the strain of the load on her head. I only hope the weight does not break her neck! At last not one but two individuals are hurrying to our home! I recognize their faces—they are among those who came to help Mother during the early days of my arrival.

The two help Mother get the load down. They are really struggling, due to the weight. Before long they have managed to get the load safely to the ground. "Hey Maame Ama, how were you able to carry such a heavy load?" one of the two helpers wants to know. "Maame Ama, think about your own health! You gave birth not long ago, so please don't overstrain yourself."

"Thanks, I just decided to carry as much as I can due to the forth-coming festivities!"

"You should have carried what you could and asked us to collect the rest. We have already told you we are ready to assist you!"

That is very nice of them. I really admire the close solidarity between residents of this community. Everyone seems to be his or her neigh-bour's keeper—really exemplary.

*

We are back at the field. The walk to the farm was unremarkable. What for God's sake is Father doing! He is standing on a wooden platform built around a huge tree! He is standing several feet above ground level. How did he manage to climb to such a height? He is holding an axe.

I cannot believe my eyes—but it is true! With the help of a hatchet axe he is trying to fell a tree, not an ordinary tree, but a really huge tree—not a type I have seen before! Is he dreaming, perhaps? How on earth can he achieve such a feat! Well, I'll keep on observing him from the safety of Mother's back and see what happens.

I am still fastened to Mother's back as we leave the area where Father is trying to fell the tree. We have moved to another piece of land. Even though I do not interact with Kwame and Kwaku directly, from their conversation I usually get an idea of what we are up to. Based on what I gleaned from their conversation, we have now visited the farmland that was cultivated the previous year. We are here to harvest foodstuffs.

*

We have returned to where Father is still occupying himself with the huge tree. He is making some progress, I should say. Judging from what is still left of the wood that he needs to cut through, he may require yet another day to complete the job.

Mother is now busily cooking lunch for the family. Mama, please hurry up! Papa no doubt will require a lot of food to replenish his lost energy and build up the energy reserves to help him complete the tedious task ahead of him.

*

Lunch is ready! Father is now on a break. He is sweating from head to toe and has taken a seat. His gaze is now directed towards me.

"Hey, little one, are you okay? Your Papa is trying to prepare the land for cultivation. You are too young to understand; still, I want to explain the process for you. Every year we have to prepare the land to grow foodstuffs for the following year. First, I clear the bush from the land—with the help of a machete. Next, I chop down some of the trees. This is what I am trying to do now. I need to fell some of the trees to permit the sun to shine directly on the crops to be planted. Otherwise they won't grow properly. Not all the trees are cut down however; we need to leave some on the field to provide shade.

"After I have chopped down the selected trees I go about with my machete to cut the branches off the fallen trees and cut them into smaller parts. They are then stacked together and left over a few days to dry. Next, I set fire to them to burn them. Finally, the crops are planted. Everything must be done before the onset of the rainy season—which provides the water needed for the crops to thrive.

"As I just mentioned, what I am telling you won't make any sense to you now. Still, I am telling you about this to prepare you for what lies ahead, my little one. One day it will be your turn to perform the task your father is engaged in. So get ready to assume your father's role one day!"

Did I hear him correctly? Will I be expected, one day, to fell such huge trees with a bare axe?! What a daunting prospect!

*

It is early in the morning of yet another day. I have already had a breastfeeding session. There is now much activity going on at home. With a broom in her hand, Mother is going about sweeping around the compound of our home. No one is free to take care of me, so I am stuck on her back.

Kwaku is cleaning the dirty cooking utensils from yesterday's evening meals. My guess is that because it turns dark very quickly after our evening meals, the cleaning is left until the next morning. The only assignment given to Kwame is for him to walk the little distance to Father's extended family home to collect his dinner dishes so Kwaku can clean them. From the look on his face as he left on the errand, he wasn't very amused. He has now returned and is hanging around idly.

*

It has been quite a while since the other members of the family finished their breakfast. I thought we would be heading for the farm again today. However, from what I have gleaned from the conversation between Kwame and Kwaku that I have reproduced below, it seems that will not be the case:

"I am happy we don't have to go to the farm today," Kwaku began.

"Why not?" Kwame wondered.

"Today is Wednesday. I thought you were aware we are not permitted to work on the field on Wednesdays?"

"Really?"

"Hey, are you not capable of keeping things in your head! We had the same conversation not long ago!"

"Sorry, I have forgotten all about it!"

"Well then, I am saying it one more time—no one in this community is permitted to work on the field on a Wednesday!"

"Why not?"

"It is taboo to do so. Anyone caught disobeying the rule can be fined by the traditional council."

"Really?"

"Yes indeed."

A short pause followed, interrupted by Kwaku.

"In my opinion, it is superfluous to threaten offenders with a fine."

"Why?"

"The answer is simple: hardly anyone will ever dream of breaking the rules!"

"Why not?"

"According to Papa, anyone who dares venture into the woods on a Wednesday could be confronted by strange looking beings, half-human, half-beast!"

"Really?"

"Yes indeed. The strange beings are said to possess red angry eyes and long sharp teeth with which they tear their human victims apart!"

"Stop it! Stop it!!" I am horrified! I don't want to carry the terrifying images into my sleep tonight!

"If you don't believe me, you can ask Father for confirmation."

*

I was thinking Mother would take some rest on the community's day of rest—but no, she has been on her feet for a good while performing various chores. For a while I gave her the needed peace. Much as I would have wished I could remain calm, unfortunately I have all of a sudden experienced a sudden tummy ache. It is a sudden spasm, as if someone is squeezing my intestines together. So, I am screaming!

"This troublesome fellow will not allow me the peace to carry on with my busy chores!" Mother bursts out. "Hey Kwabena or Kwaku, you've got to help me a bit! Come take care of your little brother!"

"Leave us alone to enjoy our football game!" They protest.

"Damn it! Football appears to be the only thing in the heads of these boys! How I wish either Kwaku or Kwabena or even both were girls! Then they would at least be helping by carrying the little one around, to give me a free hand to perform the numerous household chores." She prays fervently: "Dear God, please listen to my prayers and send me a girl the next time you decide to dispatch a baby into my home!"

I am really sorry for Mother! Too much work for one person! She is really stressed out. I will try and do the little I can to help her by refraining from crying at every little cause!

*

We are back at the field. Father is holding a bunch of wooden sticks, several dried wooden sticks bundled together. What is he doing? He is trying, I guess, to set fire to one end of the bundle. That indeed is what he has done. Yes, the one end of the wooden bundle is burning hot with flames.

Papa is now going around with the wooden torch and with it, setting fire to the dried bushes stacked together at various locations on the land being prepared for cultivation. Now I can see several fires burning simultaneously on various locations on the farm. I am concerned for Father's safety. He himself doesn't seem to be bothered, and is still going about setting fire to a few stacks of dried bush remaining on the field.

The fire is approaching ever closer to where Mother and I are. "Hey, Mother, please get me out of here. I don't want to be burnt alive!"

Was it in reaction to my appeal, or was it something she had already planned? In any case we have left the scene. I thought we were heading back home—but my joy is premature. She is now heading in a direction different from the one that leads home. If his facial expression is anything to go by, Kwame is not amused at all that we are not heading for home, but rather for what appears to be another of our farmlands.

I wish we were going home. The sun, combined with the heat from the burning field, is making me feel really exhausted. Fastened as I am to the back of Mother, the busy bee, I have no choice but to accompany her wherever she goes. After walking about ten minutes we came to a different farm of ours.

Mama has spread the cloth by which I was fastened to her back on the bare ground and placed me on it.

"Take care of your little brother, Kwame, as I harvest a ripened palm fruit just at the corner."

I am not hungry, so I will keep calm and give her the peace to do whatever she intends to accomplish.

She has placed a wooden ladder beside a tall palm tree. Kwame and I are watching. She is now climbing the ladder. One, two, three steps—up, up, up, she is climbing higher, even higher up the ladder. From my own estimation she is about three metres (ten feet) above ground.

"Stop it, stop it Mama! Don't go any further, this is very dangerous!" I am shouting in my own way, but no one seems to understand!

Ach, my heart is racing! I am very concerned for Mother's safety. She is not wearing a safety belt; there is no fall restraint in place, so one can only imagine what might happen should she miss a step, slip or lose her balance!

"Hey Mama, this is too risky! Why don't you leave the assignment for Papa!" Oh, I thought it was me alone who was concerned for her safety. Kwaku as well!

"Papa has a lot to do. If I were to wait on him, squirrels, rats, birds, etc., would come and feed on the palm fruit, leaving us with nothing."

"Then please be careful, we don't want anything untoward to happen to you!"

Mother is now in the process of cutting down the ripe palm fruit with the help of a machete.

Oh! I have just spotted a group of birds flying past, not very far above Mother's head. Were they perhaps on their way to feed on the very fruit Mother is harvesting? If that is the case, what they are beholding will surely be heart-breaking to them. They might as well be saying to each other: "The human beings are once again displaying their true selfish character!"

Mother is almost through with cutting the stalk attaching the fruit to the palm tree. Ouch! That was a narrow escape for Mother! As the last sinew was cut from the stock holding the palm fruit to the tree, it fell to the earth at a great speed. As it did so, it missed Mother's body by just a hairbreadth!

Now Mother is safely on the ground. She has placed the harvested fruit in a bamboo basket.

"Kwaku, that is the load you will be carrying home today, okay?"

"What about Kwame and yourself?"

"Why this question?"

"I'm just being inquisitive!"

"You are aware we are running low on our stock of plantains and cassava. I will quickly harvest some before we finally head for home."

*

We are now back on the field. The virgin forest has been cleared of the bushy undergrowth. The weeded bush has been burnt. The field is now ready to be planted with various kinds of crops. From the conversation that has been going on at home, I understand that the crops involved include the following— cocoa, cocoyam, corn, plantains and yams. Everyone at home, apart from me, will take an active part in the planting exercise.

Today's task involves yam planting. From what I am hearing it appears to be a tough assignment, requiring a considerable amount of manual labour. So, I am stuck to Mother's back while she is going about the task of planting the yams. This is the first time I am witnessing the process, so I want to describe what is going on.

With the help of a hoe, she is digging into the earth. My head is being tossed here and there, following the rhythmic upward and downward movements of Mother's body as she digs into the soil.

She has now dug about thirty centimetres deep into the earth. She is now digging to increase the width of the hole. The breadth of the pit now measures about half a metre.

What is she up to now? Refilling the dug-out hole with soil she has just laboriously excavated? What then was the purpose of the unearthing in the first place?

The pit is now about three quarters re-filled with earth. Oh, yet another surprise! Mother has placed a piece of yam she just collected from a pile not far from where we are and placed it into the earth. What is she doing now? She is pouring earth on the piece of yam. Burying the yam in the soil? I thought it was meant to be boiled and eaten! What will Kwaku and Kwame, devoted yam eaters that they are, make of that? So, the piece of yam is now completely buried in the earth. The dug-out hole is now covered to the level of the earth.

I thought we were done with planting that piece of yam. But no; that doesn't seem to be the case! Mother is now digging around the immediate perimeter of the covered pit. What is she up to? Well, it has now become clear to me. With the help of the excavated earth, she has created a mound rising to about thirty centimetres above the earth surface.

The task of planting the piece of yam is over. Mother has now moved a distance of about a metre away from the first mound and is repeating the whole process once more.

*

Mother has in the meantime planted about half a dozen yams in the fashion already described. Is it a result of the scorching heat? I am suddenly feeling unwell. I am not only feeling dizzy; I also feel like vomiting.

Arrgh, I am now throwing up! Poor Mother, her clothes are soiled with my vomit. "What is wrong with my boy?" she is wondering.

If only I were capable of speaking! I would urge her to take a break from the tedious work and seek shelter from the unbearable, yes oppressive heat.

Hey, she appears to have read my mind! She has indeed stopped working and taken shelter under the shade of a big tree.

I have in the meantime recovered from my nausea and vomiting. I am lying on Mother's lap and enjoying the lively song of a solitary bird perched on the branch of a tree not very far from where we are.

*

Today is reserved for the planting of cocoa seeds on the farm. Speaking of cocoa, from my own observations and also from listening to the conversation of my family members, cocoa plays a key role in the lives of residents of the village. To underline the important role of cocoa in our community I shall reproduce a conversation that transpired between Kwabena and Papa a few days ago:

"My school uniform is torn to pieces. I need a replacement."

"Wait for the cocoa harvest, my boy."

On another occasion, I heard Mother complaining that the roof of the kitchen is leaking:

"We need the problem fixed without delay." said Mother.

"We have to wait for the cocoa harvest; until then there is no money to purchase the roofing material needed for the repair." Father replied.

Cocoa indeed seems to play an important role when it comes to the finances of the family. Even as Kwaku requested a replacement for his tattered boxer-shorts to spare him the embarrassment of others seeing below his tattered pants, he was told to exercise some patience until the arrival of the cocoa harvesting season.

So today is reserved for planting cocoa seeds! In view of the key role cocoa plays in our family finances, I would have thought much more time would have been assigned to the planting of cocoa seeds. That however doesn't seem to be the case. Instead, the cocoa seeds share the same amount of time with the other crops—corn, plantain, maize, cocoyam, pepper, tomatoes, etc. If I had my own way, I would surely do things differently—but I better keep my mouth shut! They must have a good reason for doing things the way they are doing it now.

Now the planting of all the crops is completed. Based on the conversations going on among the rest of the family, the field will be left alone for a few weeks, after which we will return to check and see if everything is okay.

10

NO REST ON THE DAY OF REST

There is no work on the farm today. From the conversation going on between members of the family, today is Sunday, which is meant to be a day of rest. There is little indication though that members of the family are going to remain idle today.

I awoke from sleep not long ago. Mother has breastfed me and washed me down. Now I feel settled, so no need to disturb anyone. I am now in a good position to record what is going on around me.

A woman who appears to be about mother's age has just arrived in our compound. She is carrying on her head a large aluminium tray on which is a large aluminium bowl. Beside the bowl is a ladle. Even while she was quite a distance from our compound, I could hear her announcing at the top of her voice: "Here comes the *rice water* Mammy. Order your delicious *rice water* now!"

I thought she would keep her mouth shut once she entered our compound—but no! She keeps going on repeating her announcement, over and over again. On hearing her words, Kwame began to hop around, shouting at the top of his voice: "Mama, I want to enjoy rice water! Mama, please buy me a portion of rice water!"

"Leave me in peace!!" Mama replied. "I have no money for any rice water!"

Clearly disappointed by Mother's prompt and blunt rejection of his request, Kwame fell prostrate to the ground and began to cry.

"Please Mama," the rice-water seller urged, "buy something for him! Oh, poor him, he looks really disappointed!" Thus, she pleaded with Mama on behalf of my weeping brother.

"Sorry; I have no money to spare!"

"No worries, you can purchase on credit!"

"Well, if you are prepared to offer on credit, then go ahead. Be warned though, I don't know when I can pay you back!"

"Well, then, I will keep my product. You can hardly expect me to wake up early in the morning and put a lot of effort into preparing my produce only to dish it out for free!"

On realizing his chance of enjoying his favourite meal was slipping away, Kwame cried louder and louder.

"Please just give him a portion," Mother implored the seller. "I will pay as soon as I can!"

"What do you mean by as soon as you can?"

"In a matter of two weeks."

"I hope you keep your word."

"I will do my best."

"I will oblige; if only for the sake of the little one!"

Delighted, Kwame got up and quickly made it to the kitchen. He returned in no time with a small plastic bowl in his hands. The seller in the meantime brought down the load on her head and poured a measure of her rice porridge into his bowl. As she was about to return the measure back to its place, my immediate senior brother looked her in the eyes and muttered: "Please add a wee bit for me!"

"Hey boy, you must be happy with what you got! You've got to bear in mind that I am selling to you on credit!"

"Please!" Kwame persisted.

"Okay, here you are!" said the seller, pouring just a tiny bit more rice porridge into the bowl in Kwame's hand as she spoke.

"You are not going to enjoy it alone!" Kwaku, who had in the meantime arrived at the scene, told his junior brother.

"No, that is mine!"

"No, it is for both of us," Kwaku said to his little brother.

"Hey Kwaku, leave him alone. You go to the kitchen and fetch a bowl. I will buy some for you as well," Mother intervened.

So Kwaku also had a portion of rice porridge for breakfast.

"Please, don't dare venture on my compound any longer with your *rice water.* I have trained my children to eat *ampesi* for breakfast," Mother roared.

Well, for those who are not familiar with our cuisine, allow me to explain what *ampesis* is. I have indeed never tasted *ampesi* myself since I arrived here. Apparently, it is not suitable for me at this stage; it should indeed be obvious to me since teeth are required to chew it, and I am yet to develop teeth. The *ampesi* meal, basically, is made up of two components. The first part of the meal may consist of one or a combination of the following ingredients: plantain, yam, cocoyam and cassava. The second component is the sauce that goes with it, which on its part can be prepared with a single or a combination of the following: kontomire (leaves from the co-coyam plant), garden eggs, peanuts, tomatoes, pepper etc.

Ampesi is usually eaten at breakfast and at lunch. Fufu on its part forms our evening meal or supper. Ever since I arrived here, I have never witnessed a day that the family has had anything for breakfast and lunch apart from *ampesi.* I can thus understand why Kwame and Kwaku are so desirous of getting something for a change! For today, at least, they are privileged to enjoy something else.

*

As already mentioned, today is Sunday. There is no work on the farm. From the conversation going on, we will be heading for the Nwi River. The name is not unfamiliar to me. My senior brothers regularly fetch water from it for use at home.

What is the reason for visiting the riverside today? Well, based on the conversations going on among other members of the family, Mother will be there to wash the dirty linen of the whole family. She usually performs the assignment at home on Sundays, making use of either rainwater or water from the community water borehole which happens to be located just on the edge of the compound of our home.

It has not rained for a while, leaving the well all but dried out. So Mother is left with little option other than to carry the dirty linen to the riverside, to get it washed there. I ask myself, why doesn't she send the boys to fetch the water required for the washing rather than carry the items to the river to be washed? Well, it appears the dirty linen has piled up to the point she considers it easier to wash it directly at the riverside rather than at home.

Earlier on Kwaku was dispatched to the extended family home of Father, to collect his dirty linen. I don't understand why the duty of washing Father's dirty clothes should fall on Mother's shoulders—Mother, who is already burdened with performing various duties throughout the day! I will surely seek answers one day. For now, I can only pray for the needed strength to keep her going.

So, we are on our way to the Nwi River. We are walking along a bush path with the rest of the family walking beside us. As usual I am fastened to the back of Mother. As on all previous occasions, my two big brothers are walking ahead of us.

*

It has been a while since we arrived at the riverside. I am still fastened to Mother's back! My big brothers have disappointed her. They were supposed to look after me whilst she carried out her tedious assignment that brought us here. Kwame and Kwaku kept to the arrangement only for a short while! As they reluctantly took care of me, a woman of about Mother's age who was also hand washing her items near us, engaged Mama in conversation. For a while Mother's attention was distracted from us. That was the opportunity the two had probably been looking for.

Leaping to his feet, Kwaku began to run towards the stream, to be followed seconds later by Kwame.

"Hey Kwame, hey Kwaku, come back!" Mother shouts after them. "I asked you to take care of your little brother, so I can concentrate on the job of washing the dirty linen for everyone, including yourselves!"

"I am tired of keeping watch over him!" Kwaku shouted back. "I also want to enjoy swimming, just like my peers. He's your baby; you take care of him yourself!"

"You leave me to bear all the burden of the home alone!" Mother stated. "If I collapse and die out of exhaustion, you will be left alone with no one to take care of you!"

"You are not going to die; we are praying for you!" both boys shouted back as if with a single voice.

Realizing there was nothing she could do to change their minds, she gave up but sounded a note of caution: "You have to be careful not to tread too deeply into the river, okay?"

"No worries, we will take good care of ourselves," Kwaku shouted back. "We shall keep to the shallow area and not venture into the deep water.""

Mother is unconvinced. "Kojo Boye, please take good care of the little ones. Make sure they don't venture into the deep." She has addressed this appeal to a strongly built young man, probably in his early twenties, one of several young men enjoying a swim under the blue bright tropical sky on this sunny day.

"No worries, Mama, I will do just that!" he shouts back.

With my two brothers gone and me screaming out of fear something evil might befall me now that I am alone, Mother picks me up and fastens me to her back. So I am now once again stuck to Mother's back whilst she goes about the tedious task of hand washing dirty clothes piled up in front of her!

Mother is not alone—there are several others, mainly women, around us, doing the same thing.

*

For a while I managed to keep my composure, permitting her to go about her task in peace; but no more! Now I am getting unsettled. You may guess why—it is down to the basics—a need for milk!

How do I make her aware of my situation? Well as usual I have resorted to crying, or better still, screaming. So, I am screaming at the top of my voice. She doesn't seem to be amused. It appears she is determined to get the job done without any interruptions.

Well, I have decided to tone down my voice a bit, in my own interests—but I am really growing exhausted from the loud screaming. The heat, in the meantime, is becoming unbearable despite some occasional spells of fresh wind.

Ach! Two pretty birds have just flown over, heading towards the stream. Do they also want to have a swim? They should be careful that humans don't hunt them down. That reminds me of the other day when we were walking to one of our farms. Just as we went, Kwabena spotted a bird perched in one of the trees. He removed his catapult hung round his neck. Next, he took a stone he was keeping in a sack hung around his neck and placed it in a pouch. After stretching the plastic string to its utmost, he let go of the stone. The sudden release of the force propelled the stone forward with great speed. To the delight of Kwabena, the stone hit the target. The impact was so strong, it helped propel the poor bird some distance into the air before it finally fell to the ground!

How delighted Kwabena and the rest of the family were! I found it strange that they were rejoicing over the death of another living being. On reaching home Kwabena roasted it. He was generous; he shared the tiny bird with everyone in the home, including Papa and Mama. Thus in the end a big feast was held around a little bird!

The two birds I have just spotted might have been warned about the danger posed by the humans gathered beneath them, for they chose to fly quickly away instead of making a stop along the banks of the stream—to quench their thirst, perhaps.

*

We are now homeward bound. Mother is carrying the washed clothes on a big aluminium tray—on her head as usual. Each of my two brothers is carrying a bucket filled with water. I will try and keep my calm, to give everyone the needed peace and calm. I managed to do so for a while, mainly because sleep overcame me for a while.

We are back home. Mother the busy bee! She has not rested; instead, she is going about hanging the items she has just washed at the riverside. I am still fastened to her back. After several minutes she is done with hanging the clothes. I can only guess what Mother the workhorse intends doing next!

1P

AMAZING HAIRSTYLE FOR MAMA!

I shall now talk about Mother's amazing new hairstyle! After she had given me the usual morning washdown, she took time to breastfeed me. This time she allowed me to breastfeed over an unusually long period of time. The glutton that I am, I continued sucking on her nipple till I realized there was no more space in my tummy for any additional milk.

Was it intentional? To feed me to the very fullest so as to give sleep the opportunity to take control over me for the time required for what she was about to engage in? Well initially things went according to plan for her, for shortly after the feeding session was over, I dozed off.

I have no idea how long I slept. On waking up I realized I was lying alone in the bed of our room. No sooner had I woken up than I realised I had soiled my body. Initially the irritation was bearable. Soon it became uncomfortable to bear.

I do not want to dwell on my well-known method of drawing attention to my plight so as to avoid unnecessary repetition.

"Kwame, please go check on your brother!"

"Me again!"

"Please! Just go and keep him company. Hopefully your presence will give him the reassurance he needs to keep calm."

"You must know him well enough to realize he only keeps quiet when you are around!"

"Just give it a try. Aunty Yaa Yaa has taken time off to help plait my hair. She is almost through with it. I don't want to interrupt her."

Kwame has burst into my room. "You keep your mouth shut crybaby, or I'll show you the red card!"

"Kwame, don't shout at him. Just keep him company!" Mother's intervention is very prompt.

"Yes, Mama!"

Kwame has sat down near me. He is rubbing his palm tenderly on my forehead. I am not impressed by his attempt to soothe me. Instead of calming down, I continue to scream louder and louder. After trying in vain to calm me, Kwame's facial expression suggests his patience is wearing thin.

"Shut up boy! I cannot bear any more of this!" Ah! My brother has exploded at last!

"Hey Kwame, don't scream at him! It will only make matters worse!"

"Okay then little Prince, I cannot bear your shrieks any longer! I am gone!" Oh! he did not mince his words—he *is* gone! Well, I have no choice but to escalate matters so I am yelling even louder—notwithstanding that my cries are exhausting!

*

At last mother has entered the room. I can hardly recognize her! The hair on one part of her head has been plaited into locks, while nothing has happened to the hair on the other half of her head. I have stopped crying out of wonder and amazement at Mother's new looks. Mother has noticed that and won't let it go without a comment.

"Hey Yaa Yaa, just take a look! The boy is so surprised by my new look that he has stopped crying abruptly and is staring at me instead of crying!"

My caring mother has cleaned me and changed my clothes. I have also been breastfed. She has now turned to me:

"Kofi, I am going to fasten you to my back. Please be quiet for a while to give Aunty the needed peace to turn me into a real princess."

So, I'm once again fastened to Mother's back. Aunty has resumed the plaiting of Mother's hair. I'm observing the process at close range. I will describe it as best as I can.

With the help of a wooden comb, the hairdresser has separated a small portion of the hair from the main bulk. She is holding the portion so separated in one hand. Making use of the other hand, she has picked out a thin black thread—one of several of its kind lying on a small table close to Mama. Starting from the base of the separated hair on the head upwards, she is tying a thin thread around the hair. She has now got to the very top of the plaited hair bundle. I am paying close attention. What is she up to? Well, she has tied the thread into a knot at the very apex of the plaited hair bundle. Job done!

Aunty is repeating the procedure all over again. Step by step, she is going about the task of plaiting Mother's hair. About half an hour since I began observing the process, Aunty is left with the very last portion of hair to be plaited. The job is soon completed—every portion of hair is plaited! I just wonder what Aunty's next step will be.

I am still paying close attention! Aunty has now begun weaving the plaited hair—about half a dozen on one half of the head—together. She does the same for the other side. What a gorgeous hairstyle it has turned out to be! Mama is looking indeed like a charming Queen.

I can't help asking myself, how will she manage to balance items on her head with this hairdo? Well, she will surely find a way, considering that carrying items on the head is part and parcel of her existence.

And then I do ask myself—will I also have to display such hairstyles in the future? Time will tell.

1Q

THE CARING "SISTERS" AND THEIR HAPPY PATIENT

The days have been turning into nights, to be followed by more days; I have been counting them! I think today is day thirty-five of my arrival here—I may not be very accurate with that figure though.

I don't know what is going on. My body seems unable to store milk anymore. No sooner have I sucked some into my belly than everything comes out from below. Moments later, whatever might have still been left in my belly comes out of the mouth.

The condition has persisted for three days. I feel so drained. My body is also feeling hot; sometimes it feels as if I am on fire. At the beginning of my troubles, I still managed to drink Mother's sweet and tasty milk. That has changed. Indeed, since yesterday, the milk has not only lost its taste, it has also turned bitter—which has led me to stop drinking. I am now feeling weaker and weaker. What is to be done? I have no idea.

*

It is early in the morning. I have been visited by a tall elderly person. His face is familiar. Oh! I recall him. He was one of the individuals who attended to Mother on the day I emerged from her body. I wonder what he is up to.

Now I know! He unzipped a bag hanging on his shoulders, and pulled out a bottle containing a brown coloured liquid. He has now turned to Mother: "This is good medicine for his condition. Give him two teaspoons three times daily—morning, afternoon and evening. You should notice some improvement in due time," he says. "I will come back and check on him tomorrow. You should of course feel free to contact me in case his condition deteriorates."

*

It is evening. I am still feeling awful, I am so weak, I am left with hardly any energy to even cry. I really doubt if the medicine will make any difference.

*

Ah! I have just thrown up. Since I have not been drinking, I can only wonder where that fluid comes from. It may well be the very last drops of fluid still remaining in my body.

Now Papa and Mama are engaged in a conversation; I am paying close attention to the dialogue:

"We need to take him to hospital, otherwise we might lose him!" That was Mama.

'Lose him?' To whom? I have no idea. I will continue to pay close attention to what they're saying.

"Yes, I agree with you," says Papa. "We need to take him to hospital without delay. I am just wondering where we can find the needed cash. You are aware of our financial situation."

"We will have to take a loan," Mother has suggested.

"Yes I agree with you," Papa replies. "Even if that implies us having to pledge one of our farms to secure the loan. We will have to do whatever it takes to avoid the worst-case scenario."

'The worst-case scenario?' What does he mean by that? How I do indeed wish I could interact with them directly! Papa and Mama! They appear cash-strapped all the time! Even when their baby is very unwell, they are still struggling to come up with the funds needed to take him to hospital!

*

Well, it appears, they managed to find someone to lend them the money. So Mother is getting ready to take me to hospital. Hospital? What is that? Well, I guess it's a place they take children like myself to who are unwell. Mother's preparation has caught Kwame's attention.

"Mama, why are you putting on your tidy clothes?"

"I am taking your brother to the Hospital."

"Hospital?"

"Yes, he is not feeling well."

"Where then?"

"The Roman Catholic Hospital at Nkawkaw."

"May I come along?"

"No, you will stay behind. The hospital is a place where we take those who are not feeling well. You look strong and energetic."

*

We have been waiting on the roadside for a while—awaiting a vehicle to take us to Nkawkaw. From what I have gleaned from the conversation going on, our destination is about 20 miles (30km) away.

The first vehicle that went by was a wooden truck, filled to the last available space with passengers! Some were even standing on the tail-board whilst yet more of the travellers were lying on the roof of the vehicle.

At long last a vehicle has pulled to a stop. It is also full. I wonder where we can find a space. Well, fortunately, a few passengers have alighted from it, so there should be some space left for us. Mother has handed me to a stranger to help her climb onto the vehicle.

It is a huge truck endowed with two cabins. The front cabin is small and built with metal. It is occupied by the driver and two passengers. The second cabin where we are crammed into can be described as a huge wooden cage. Within it, arranged in rows of about seven, are long wooden seats. I am not exaggerating, but it is really overcrowded; I guess it is carrying about double the number of passengers it is officially permitted to transport.

I am crying in protest, for being handed to this stranger. She is smiling; to be fair to her she appears very friendly to me. Nevertheless, I am not impressed—still yelling at the top of my voice! It is a real strain on me—the screaming, but she is not perturbed.

I can at last breathe a sigh of relief—the stranger has handed me back to Mother. She has already found a place. I am now lying on her lap. The vehicle is now fully packed with passengers—quite unsuitable to carry a sick and frail child.

Oh! I thought there was no more space in the wooden vehicle for additional passengers! But no, someone has just climbed on board. And guess what? That individual has been directed by the driver's assistant to sit on our seat—the seat which can barely offer space for those already seated on it!

"Can you please push and squeeze a bit together to create some space for him!" the driver's mate pleads with those on that row.

"Push to where; to the heavens?" protests a sharp-tongued lady seated next to Mother.

"Didn't your parents teach you how to talk politely!" the driver's assistant bursts out.

"Hey, you teenage rascal, mind how you talk to the elderly!" a person sitting in front of us, not directly affected by the problem, has cried out.

"Calm down everyone. Let's keep calm and ask Almighty God to bring us safely to our respective destinations."

Can you guess who just spoke? Mother! She is the only one who has remained calm in the highly charged atmosphere. Her words seem to have done the trick. Everyone has calmed down and heeded the instruction to squeeze up a bit more closely to each other. That has resulted in a tiny space being created and the newcomer has squeezed himself into the space.

*

The vehicle has now been set in motion. It can only move at what can be described as a snail's pace along the dusty road. Ach, the wind has blown a trail of dust into the vehicle. I can hear a couple of the passengers coughing. I am thankful that I am not choked to death by the dust before reaching the hospital.

Ouch, that hurts! Someone has accidentally crushed his elbow into my head! I don't blame the individual concerned; it was caused by a sudden and violent bump of the vehicle which resulted in the passengers being tossed about. Ach! Yet another loud bang—really violent! My bones might well be crushed to pieces before we reach our destination.

*

I thought this vehicle would travel a bit faster but no, that is not the case; we are making very slow progress. Not only is it moving at a snail's pace, it is also pulling to a stop at almost every small hamlet along the way to allow passengers to get off and others to climb on board.

My goodness! Yet another violent shaking of the vehicle. Mother had to hold on tightly onto me. Thank goodness she did not lose her grip on me. I might otherwise have fallen to the floor, risking being trampled to death by one or more of my fellow passengers! Mama can prevent me from falling, but she cannot prevent me from throwing up. The violent shaking has resulted in fluid being ejected from my stomach. Oh, this is embarrassing! The vomit soils not only Mother's clothing but also that of a gentleman sitting next to her.

"Apologies, my dear," Mama has told him.

I expected him to be very cross, but no! Surprisingly, he doesn't seem bothered!

"Don't worry, Mama, it is not your fault. I also have a baby girl, just about the same age as yours."

"Thanks for your understanding."

"A boy or a girl?" he inquires, his gaze fixed on me.

"A boy. I have a total of five boys. Including his father, I have a total of six males to contend with alone at home."

"That must be a really difficult call!"

"That is exactly the case. I am hoping for a girl next time to offer me the much-needed assistance."

"Oh, so the game is not over yet?" he laughs.

"No, not until I get a girl!"

"Well, I can only wish you all the best."

"Thanks, my dear."

*

The vehicle has pulled to a halt again. I have lost count of the number of times it has so far stopped. It appears to be the end of its journey, for everyone is climbing down. A young lady who seems to be in a hurry is not waiting for Mother to climb down before her. Instead, she is squeezing herself through the little space between Mother and the row ahead of us.

"Ouch!" Mother exclaims. "Lady, you have stepped on my feet! Why the rush?"

"Sorry, Ma'am. I am here for an interview. I left home very early, but now I am almost an hour late!"

"Well, all the best; hope you get the job!"

"Thanks."

Almost everyone has got down. Mother and a few other mums with babies like me are still on board. How is Mother going to climb down from this wooden vehicle with me on her lap? She has passed me on to a stranger—to enable her to climb down, I suppose. I am concerned she is leaving me alone! I scream aloud in protest. Everyone around looks in my direction.

Mother has now stepped out of the vehicle. The stranger is now lowering me down, into Mother's arms.

"Hey, please be careful you don't drop me to the bare ground!" I yell. "I want to keep all my bones intact"! Thank goodness I have landed safely in Mother's arms. Mother has once again, skilfully, I must add, performed the usual manoeuvre that restores me at her back. With the help of a piece of java print which I suppose she carried along for the very purpose, I am now fastened to her back.

Maybe Father should have accompanied us. His assistance would have spared her some of the hassle. From the conversation he had with mother prior to our departure it was clear to me that he has to be on the field to perform some important duties—chores that need doing today.

So we are on the street of this strange town. It is no doubt far larger than our little village. I can see many more of these four-wheeled devices, moving up and down. Why are they hooting and honking so loudly? Can't they drive to their destinations without resorting to such loud noises?

Ouch! That was close. Now I understand why the vehicles are hooting loudly. A young boy just as big as Kwaku has some items on his head. I think he is trying to sell them. I think he was desirous of catching up with a vehicle parked on the other side of the road—but he crossed the road without paying attention. It is only the loud hooting of the vehicle that drew his attention to the danger. It is really loud everywhere on the street.

Most of those on the street are carrying objects on their heads—most of them are shouting at the top of their voices, perhaps to draw attention to what they are offering for sale. But is anyone taking any notice of them? They may well lose their voices if they spend the whole day shouting and yelling in such a manner.

Some of the people on the street are not only bearing loads on their heads but also on their shoulders. Some of the women have gone a step further—they are not only bearing loads on their heads and shoulders, but also carrying babies on their backs!

We have left the main road and are now walking on a road branching from the main road. It is quieter here; nothing approaching the hustle and bustle I have just referred to. After walking on this quieter road for about ten minutes, we find it ends in a cul-de-sac.

We have left the road and are now walking on a footpath. Just ahead of us, not far from where the road comes to an end, is a large gate leading to a large compound. The security has allowed us through. It's much quieter here.

After walking a few minutes along the cemented lane leading from the gate, we enter the gate of a large building. We have come to a stop. Mother is exchanging words with a lady wearing a green uniform. She has something hanging around her neck. Ouch! Mother has handed me to the stranger.

I am protesting by way of screaming. The lady, instead of reciprocating my unfriendly behaviour towards her and walking away, doesn't seem to be offended. Instead, she is showing me a very friendly face. Oh, what a gorgeous smile she has! Shame on me for behaving so rudely towards her.

She is now addressing mother; I will pay attention.

"Mama, your baby is very dehydrated. His problem without doubt began some time ago! We have all the time been advising you mothers to bring your children and babies to our attention at the first sign of disease. But no, you don't seem to understand simple instructions! Instead, you keep them at home and seek help only when it is almost too late!"

The stranger seems very concerned about me. I'm dehydrated! ? What does she mean by that? What a pity I am unable to communicate with her directly! Mother feels a bit embarrassed. For a while she seems unable to say anything to counter the claims levelled against her. Well, now she is about to speak, I am keen to hear what she has to say:

"Sister, it is not our fault. We have in the Twi language the saying: 'You may find something attractive, but without money you cannot purchase it!' What should I make of your proverb, dear Mother—yes I call you Mother because you could as we'll be my mother."

"Well," the Sister answered, "I just wanted to make it clear to you that we would have wished you had come earlier, and understand that the lack of money has delayed you. But we don't charge much; indeed, our fees are very heavily subsidized by the government."

"Unfortunately," Mother replied, "that is still a considerable sum of money for our lean purse. You should also bear in mind that we had to pay for the transportation."

"I have heard such stories over and over again. You mothers have money for other matters, such as purchasing new clothes for every funeral. Yet when it comes to the health of your children, you play the poverty card!"

"Sorry, Sister. Please do what you can to help my little one."

"Of course, we will do our best. He is not only dehydrated, meaning he has hardly any fluids in his body; he also has a very high temperature. You take a seat. Someone will attend to you without delay."

We are seated in the waiting room. I am really sorry for Mother. She does not deserve the rebuke after all she has been doing for me under very challenging circumstances. We are not the only ones in the waiting room; there are about a dozen others, including babies like me.

*

After waiting for a while Mother has been asked to proceed to a room. There are two ladies in the room. One is wearing a green uniform just like the one worn by the lady we met earlier on; nothing unusual about her. Not so the other lady in the room. Not only is she dressed differently (she is dressed in a white uniform), the colour of her skin is very pale, not like anything I have ever seen. Her hair is also silky, not like the coarse black hair I am used to. Hey, what kind of human being is this? Or is she perhaps a ghost or a visitor from a different world? The manner in which the strange individual speaks is also different from anything I am conversant with. The way she speaks leads me to suspect she might be speaking from her nose!

The strange looking individual has taken hold of me. Ouch! She has ripped me naked—I feel really embarrassed to be so exposed to strangers. Well, she appears to be very concerned for my wellbeing, so let her do as she deems fit.

She is now examining me; I am being checked from head to toe. First, she has felt almost every part of my body making use of both palms. Next, she is using an instrument that has hung around her neck to examine me.

The examination has taken quite a while. It is now over, I guess. She has now turned to Mother:

"We have to keep your baby here for a few days," she begins.

"No, please! I have other little children at home to care for."

"Madam, you should first consider the welfare of your little one! He is very unwell. It is good you brought him in today—tomorrow would have been too late."

"Of course, the welfare of my little one takes preference over everything else. There is a problem though."

"What problem?"

Mother appears hesitant. I hope she is not going to mention money, lack of money to be specific.

"Madam please be quick. We have several other patients to see."

"Madam, unfortunately I was only given just enough money to bring him to your attention. The money I have left is just enough to pay for the return journey."

"Madam, we can discuss the issue of money later. We are morally bound to help this little one. It will be unethical on our part to refuse him treatment on monetary grounds. So, just follow the nurse to the ward."

*

We arrived in a large hall. I can see several beds. They are not empty but occupied by little children just as big as me. Their mothers are standing or sitting near them. Some are settled, others are crying at the top of their voices. There are several ceiling fans blowing air down—really refreshing air.

*

I have been placed in a bed—a really soft and comfortable bed; nothing like the one I am used to. This is for me alone. What a privilege to have my own bed; no need to share with anyone.

Talking of sharing a bed with others, I am reminded of an incident I experienced some time ago. As already mentioned, I share the same bed with my parents. The other day Father, very deeply asleep, moved his hands around hitting me on the head as a result. Ouch! It was so painful and I began to yell at the top of my voice. My screams awakened Mother.

"What is wrong with you, my little one?"

I kept screaming.

"Hey Koogyamfi, did you hit him in your sleep?" she queried

No reply!

Mother repeated the question.

Still no reply. Father appeared to be far, far away from both of us.

Now at last, I have a whole bed for myself—no need to fear the prospect of someone hitting me in their sleep.

Ah! I don't have to be so self-centred, considering only my welfare. If I am sleeping alone in my bed, where can Mother sleep? Of course, even if I wanted to offer her a place, it wouldn't be possible due to the small size of the bed. I guess it was specially made for kids.

*

The Sisters—well, I hope that is how they are called for everyone is calling them by that name—are occupied taking care of the kids in their care. Two of them are taking care of me as I lie on Mother's lap.

A third person has just arrived with a tray in hand. She has handed it to one of the two Sisters. Ouch! That hurts! One of them has injected something into my left arm! It hurts; yes indeed it does! How dare they inflict such pain into a little one in their care! I thought initially they were trying to help me. Now I get the impression they are out to terrorize me! But that cannot be the case because they are smiling in a friendly manner at me. One of them has even picked up a tissue and is tenderly wiping away the tears from my face.

I cannot understand the paradox—on the one hand appearing very friendly, and on the other hand the willingness to inflict pain on me! Well, maybe I am too young to understand!

One of the nurses arrives carrying in one hand a plastic bottle filled with clear fluid. A thin plastic tube is attached to the tip of the bottle. The end of the tube has been attached to a small line left in my left arm. Oh, it appears they want to give me some fluid. That is very kind of them. I am indeed grateful to them for the effort they have so far undertaken to help me regain my health.

*

Poor Mother. If the expression on her face is anything to go by, she appears to be confused indeed! I guess she is thinking about the rest of the family. She may be wondering how Kwame and Kwaku can cope without her? I don't think she reckoned with my admission. I really wonder how she can pass the message on to Father and the rest. Father will surely be concerned about the same way mother is also worried about them.

Me the trouble maker! I am really sorry for the rest of the family, for bringing them into such a situation!

*

I am tired; and want to go to bed. Poor mother, where will she sleep? All the beds in the room are just as small as mine, not big enough for her. Ach; as if the Sisters were reading my mind. Just the moment those thoughts were going through my mind, two of them arrived carrying a big mattress. They have placed it on the bare floor, just near my bed.

"Mama, this is your bed. We will be back soon with a pillow and the dressing." They have been true to their words and returned after a short while. They have dressed the bed for Mother.

Mother is now asleep. Ach, she is snoring, quite loudly! I hope no one here complains about the noise.

I don't know how long we are going to remain here. For now, however, I am enjoying my stay here. Good night, everyone!

*

Hey, it is morning! I really enjoyed the night—no mosquitoes to disturb my sleep.

Surprise, surprise! I can see Father! How did he get here so quickly? He is conversing with Mother. I will pay attention.

"I couldn't sleep the whole night! I went to check on any vehicle that pulled to a stop to see whether you were in it. To no avail. How I wish there was any way I could communicate with you! Well, on getting up, I joined the next available commuter vehicle and headed for here." Father has now turned his attention to me. "Kofi, my dear, how are you doing? You will surely make it, thanks to the professional care of the amazing staff!"

I can only agree with him. The whole hospital staff, the cleaners, the nurses, the doctors—they have all been very caring and very loving.

*

I think Papa is preparing to leave. He is engaged in conversation with the staff so I will pay attention.

"Thank you very much for your help. Can I please know when he will be discharged?"

"We want to keep him here for at least three more days. He was very dehydrated—oh, how can I explain dehydration to your understanding? I mean at the time of his arrival here his body had lost a considerable amount of fluid. We require a few more days to refill him. Hope that explanation is clear."

"Yes, I think so. I am an illiterate small peasant farmer. I am at home with matters pertaining to tilling the land, harvesting food-crops, hunting for wild game, etc. Nothing with medical terms!"

So Father has left. I am left with Mother and the loving staff.

The thought of enjoying this wonderful environment for at least three more days is really reassuring. If I had my own way I would stay here indefinitely and not return home—not back to the disturbing mosquitoes, the naughty *baa, baas;* the silly *maa maas* and the cacophony of noises that disturb my peace, not only during the day, but also during the night!

And my brothers? Will they miss me? Will I miss them? Well, I may eventually miss them; for now, however, that is not the case.

*

It appears our stay here is over! Mama has packed everything into her bag. If that is the case, that is no good news for me! Indeed, I wish we could make it our home.

Hello, I have an idea! One day, when I am big enough to travel on my own, I will come back and plead with them to permit me to work here. I will accept anything they can offer—cleaner, gardener, dish-washer—for a change.

Well, it is surely over. Mother has picked up her bag. We are now surrounded by the friendly hospital staff who have been dealing with me so far. Oh, I can see the tears dropping from the eyes of some of them.

"Goodbye sweet little Kofi, we shall miss you," one of them says. I guess she is the team leader.

"Goodbye dear Kofi. Keep healthy so you don't have to come back," another has remarked

Oh! I don't want to say Amen to that. I will surely want to come back and enjoy their wonderful services and kindness—as early as tomorrow if I had my own way!

We have now left the building—the building that served as my home for the past few days—and are heading back home.

*

We are back home. We went through an almost identical ordeal on the return journey—with one exception. As we got to the station to board a vehicle, Mama all of a sudden cried in excitement: "Hey KK, what are you doing here?"

"This is my vehicle."

"Your vehicle? How did my dear cousin come by the considerable sum needed to purchase such a vehicle?"

"No, it is not my property," he smiles. "It belongs to my master. I earn a daily wage for driving it. So from henceforth, with the exception of Sundays, I will be driving through your village on my round trip from my home at Akim Swedru to Nkawkaw and back."

"You should make a short stopover to say hello to your favourite cousin whenever your time permits!"

"Yes, I will. By the way, what brings you to Nkawkaw?"

"I brought my little one to the hospital. He spent five days in the children's ward. He has just been discharged."

"What was wrong with him?"

"He had a high temperature; he was also not drinking."

"Malaria, perhaps?"

"Yes, that is what the doctors told me. Thank goodness he has recovered."

"Okay, you will occupy the front cabin. Though it is already occupied, I will explain the situation to those occupying it and ask them to move to the back."

So we were privileged to travel in the front cabin! Though the vehicle had to travel slowly on the rugged road, I was spared the pushing and squeezing I was subjected to on the earlier journey. So I am back safely home.

Hardly back home and I am already yearning to go back where we came from.

*

It has been a few days since we returned home. I am feeling stronger with every passing day. Breast milk is tasting as delicious as it used to prior to our journey to hospital. I am grateful to all who have helped restore me to good health.

1R

HOME TURNED INTO A FAST-FOOD RESTAURANT

As on several previous occasions, I am fastened to Mother's back. It is quite early in the morning, not yet daybreak. I woke up from sleep not long ago. I turned around. Neither Mama nor Papa were around. I was scared to the bones. I began screaming at the top of my voice.

Moments later Mama arrived:

"I thought you had left me in peace to prepare the *kotonte* meal," Mama said. "I must get it ready to serve to the public before daybreak. We desperately need the little income to be earned to help keep our heads above water financially! I am behind schedule; the first customers will arrive any moment—so you shut up cry-baby!"

So saying, she got hold of me, bent down a little bit and performed the usual manoeuvre the reader is now familiar with. So now I am tightly fastened to Mama's back. Just as she stepped out of the room, the "*koo-koo kooh!*" The sound of a cockerel reached my ears. I could sense the approaching arrival of daybreak, though it was still quite dark.

*

Mama is now in the process of preparing a *kokonte* meal. I am hearing the term *kokonte* for the first time. I will pay attention and describe the process as clearly as I can.

A large aluminium cooking dish filled halfway with water is set on a crude, makeshift clay stove in the middle of our compound. The water has just begun to boil. With one hand, Mother is pouring an ash-looking

105

meal into the boiling water; she has a wooden ladle in her other hand with which she is quickly stirring the powder being poured into the hot water.

Surprise, surprise! The moment the white-to-ash coloured meal mixes with the boiling water, it assumes a light brown colour! How is that possible? That is one of the first questions I will ask Mother when I am able to speak.

I am feeling the heat, both from the steam and the open fire. I blame myself! If I had remained settled in bed and refrained from causing a commotion, I would have remained peaceful in bed. I really want to be sent back to bed. But how can I make the matter clear to Mama? May crying help convey the message? Well, I will give it a try. So I am crying at the top of my voice.

"Hey, you better shut up there! You should have kept quiet and slept in your comfortable bed instead of causing a stir!" Ouch, my action has had the opposite effect! Mother has referred to our bed as "comfortable"—comfortable, really?

*

For quite a time Mother has been stirring the brown-coloured mixture that has changed into a semi-solid consistency. All this time she has been stirring, my head was being tossed here and there following her body movements. I guess food is now ready to be served, for she has stopped stirring. What is she doing now? I am still paying attention!

She has collected a large aluminium bowl. With the help of the ladle and a small plate, she is cutting and forming the food into small ready-to-serve portions. I now understand why Mother spent quite a while in the kitchen the previous evening before retiring to bed. Fortunately for her, I was settled lying on the bed with Kwaku babysitting so she was left in peace to accomplish what she was engaged in.

Now it is clear to me what exactly she was engaged in—preparing the soup needed to serve the *kokonte*. From what I have just learnt from a conversation between Mama and Kwaku, just as in the case of fufu, one requires soup to swallow down the *kokonte* balls. Today, Mama will serve *kokonte* with peanut soup 'to go'.

*

It is now daybreak.

"*Kokonte*! Delicious *kokonte* is ready to serve!" Mother keeps shouting at the top of her voice. I guess she is inviting customers to come and purchase a meal.

The message seems to have got around, for residents have started arriving at our compound. Some are coming empty handed; others have little bowls in their hands. I guess those carrying their bowls are coming to purchase to take away. Meanwhile my two other brothers have woken up.

"Hey tasty *kokonte*, I want a portion of tasty *kokonte* to enjoy straight away!" That is Kwame jumping and hopping around. He seems really excited, creating the impression he will be tasting a meal of *kokonte* for the first time!

Mother has turned to both: "Hey boys, both of you, run to the street and cry aloud: '*Kokonte, kokonte*, tasty *kokonte* is ready to serve!' Quick, both of you!"

Meanwhile several additional customers have arrived to purchase delicious *kokonte* for breakfast.

Mother is serving a customer. I will pay attention:

She has placed two slices of *kotonte* into a bowl. Next, she poured full ladles of soup into the bowl. The customer has also ordered a piece of *tilapia*, which Mother has served.

Mother has now handed the order to the customer. She has now stretched her hand to demand payment.

"Sorry, Mama, no cash today!"

No cash today? Did I hear him right?

Mother is clearly upset. "Why didn't you make that clear to me at the beginning? I have decided not to sell on credit anymore."

"Sorry, Mama. I will be harvesting my cocoa beans next week. I will pay you as soon as I receive payment for my product."

I thought he would be the last person to purchase on credit. But no, that is not the case—and at least half a dozen other customers did likewise. That doesn't sound encouraging! Indeed, after all the effort Mama invested in getting the meal ready, I expected every buyer to make immediate payment.

Oh! I just remembered that Mother also purchased *koko* on credit the other day! Buying on credit appears to be a normal way of doing business in this community!

1 S

DRAINING STREAMS FOR A DAILY BREAD

Mother has finished her early morning chores. I thought she would rest awhile, but no, she has fetched a large aluminium basket from the kitchen and placed it on the open ground of the compound. Next, she has packed about half a dozen plastic and aluminium bowls, part of our household utensils, into the basket. What is she up to? Oh, I will pay attention, for she is now addressing my two brothers:

"Get ready you boys, we will be going out soon!"

"Going out soon?" Kwakwu is looking up to her. I can read the surprise written on his face.

"Yes, we will soon be heading for the woods?"

"For the woods? I thought today was a rest day!"

"Who told you so?"

"Sunday has always been a day of rest!" Kwame has joined in the conversation.

"Sorry, we cannot stay at home today."

"Why not?" Kwame wants to know

"We need to find fish for our fufu meal! We have a good stock of plantains and cassava to prepare the fufu balls. What we are short of is the meat or fish needed to prepare the soup to go with the fufu balls."

"The solution is simple—ask Papa for money to purchase dry fish from the local fish-sellers." Good one, Kwame!

"Didn't you hear the conversation I had with him a short while ago?"

"No, I was not paying attention. What did he say?"

"No cash left!"

"Really?"

"Yes indeed. So we are going on an *ahweye* expedition. Hopefully we will be blessed with a good catch of fish to last us several days."

"*Ahweye* expedition? No, please count me out!" Kwaku states categorically.

"No, everyone at home is coming along!"

"My goodness! We have to accompany you to work on our various farmlands Mondays to Saturdays? I thought we could rest on a Sunday. But no, we are being asked to accompany you on an *ahweye* expedition—which implies another day of hard labour!" Kwaku is really frustrated.

"Do you think I am doing this for fun? No, I, too, am exhausted to the very bones. I wish I could stay at home and relax my bones, but there is no way out!"

"Gosh, why did I end up in this village? If ever I am given the chance to return to the world, I will stay far, far away from this little settlement with the big name Mpintimpi."

"Well, Kwaku, it is too late—you have to find a way of surviving the present. Do you think I deliberately opted for poverty and deprivation? Of course I also wish I was not born to poor parents. I thought I would get a wealthy gentleman to marry me. But no, fate brought me to someone who is as poor as I am. In the end both of us had to start from scratch."

Kwaku will not let the matter rest! "I don't blame you for our predicament. Nevertheless, I have already made up my mind. Next time I am told to proceed to the two impoverished individuals by the name of Kofi Gyamfi and Amma Owusuah, residents of a little village in rural Ghana, I will politely decline the offer!"

"Well, for now you have been sent to us, so we have to find a way to survive."

*

After about half an hour's walk on a pathway through the woods we arrive at the banks of a stream. I cannot see any bridge anywhere; I am wondering how we are going to cross over to the other side. Ah, it appears our journey has ended here. How do I know? Well Mother has put down the large tray she had been carrying. What is she up to? I can only wonder.

"Kwame, find a place to sit. You are too young to help build the dam; Kwaku, come along and help build it."

Building a dam? What is a dam? Well, I will pay attention and observe everything closely.

With the help of a machete mother cuts down some of the young plants growing along the banks of the stream. She has now gathered quite a heap of wood. Next, she and my brothers carry the wood to the stream. Mother places the wood in the river, directly across the riverbed. What is she hoping to achieve? Stop the flow of the stream, perhaps? That will require a great deal more wood! Do we have the time required to achieve that today? Well, I will keep reporting on their progress.

A good while since they went to work, they have managed to pile up several pieces of wood across the riverbed—not on a single location as I originally thought. No, there are two piles at a distance of about twenty metres from each other. Though the piles of wood have managed to slow down the flow of water at the respective sites, they have not succeeded in completely interrupting the flow.

I am still observing the course of events. What is Mother up to now? She has picked up the steel garden hoe she carried along on the aluminium tray and has begun excavating soil from a location just near the river bank! After being at work for a while, she has managed to excavate a heap of soil rising quite a distance above the ground.

Mother has stopped digging now. She has taken a seat on a wooden bench just near the heap of dug-out soil. She appears really worn out. Has she got the strength to carry on? I just wonder!

Well, apparently she still has some energy reserves, for she is back on her feet after resting for only a short while. She is now filling three bowls we brought along with a portion of the excavated soil. She has placed a bowl on the head of each of my brothers. She has now lifted the third bowl onto her head. They walk the short distance to the pile of wood at the upstream end of the river bed. One after the other, they have dumped the soil over the pile of wood. What are they aiming to achieve? Block the flow of the stream? Will that be possible? Well, I will keep watching.

The three have gone back to collect more soil which they have once more dumped on the pile of wood. This back-and-forth procedure has been going on for a while. I thought they would grow weary of this, but no, they have persisted.

Wow, their effort has been rewarded! Yes, contrary to my expectations, they have indeed succeeded in damming the river bed at that spot!

Now they have turned their attention to the pile of wood at the downstream end. Assisted by my two dutiful brothers, mother is now attempting to dam that site as well. I want to avoid repetition, so will desist from engaging in another running commentary! I will keep my mouth shut for a while and watch and see what happens.

I am back reporting! I am happy to announce that after several minutes of concerted effort from the three workers, the second dam is completed.

I am curious to know Mother's next step. She has just instructed my two brothers to join her at the front side of the downstream dam. She has handed each of the two a medium-sized bowl. She has a far larger one in her hands.

So, the three are lined up in front of the downstream dam—Kwaku to the left, mother in the middle, Kwame to the right. One, two, three... off they go! Working in sync, they dip the bowls into the water, fill them up and then pour the water over the dam. It appears they are attempting to bail out the demarcated section of the stream of the water trapped in there. If that indeed happens to be their objective, then we may well spend the night here!

The three have been on the job for a good while. Even from a distance, I can tell from the facial expressions of my two brothers that they are yearning for a break. Mother on her part appears so absorbed in the assignment that she seems to have forgotten everyone else.

*

Goodness me, I am beginning to feel hungry. Mother is so absorbed in her task that she may even have forgotten about me! I better draw her attention to my predicament or risk starving to death! So, I have resorted to the familiar method of making her aware that not everything is okay with me.

"Stop crying, my little one! Just bear with me for a short while; I need to maintain the momentum!"

Bear with her? For how long? I am not impressed—still yelling at the top of my voice.

"Kwame, Kwaku, carry on with the good work! I need to pause a while to breastfeed your little brother."

"I also need a break! I am exhausted!" Kwaku declares.

"Me too!" Kwame concurs.

My two brothers should thank me for helping them get their much-deserved breaks that followed my intake of welcome milk!

*

So, the team is on a break! They have just finished eating the *ampesi* meal mother had brought along. As they started the meal my two brothers complained that it had turned cold. Nevertheless, they wolfed the whole meal down in no time!

Having breastfed me, Mother no doubt will be glad if I am able to close my eyes in sleep, to give her a free hand to carry on with the task she has set herself. For some reason I am still awake—not only awake, but also quite unsettled—from a cramping tummy!

"Boys, let's get back to work," Mother issues the order.

"But Kofi is still awake; who will take care of him?"

"I will fasten him to my back."

"Fasten him to the back and drain the stream at the same time?"

"Well, there is no choice. I cannot afford to leave him in Kwame's care. It is getting late—we need all hands-on deck to quickly drain the stream and get back home before the fall of darkness."

So break over, work has resumed.

The team perseveres in their effort to drain the water from the demarcated section of the stream. I am now waiting to see what happens from an even closer range. It is without doubt a really laborious undertaking! I can only wish them the best of luck, indeed that their painstaking endeavour is rewarded with a good catch.

*

Though the sun is shining, happily there are several trees growing along the banks of the stream—offering the needed shade for us all. If that were not the case the exposure to the direct sunshine and remorseless heat of the sun would have been overwhelming.

It has been quite a while since the team resumed work. Is it a fantasy or reality? I think it's reality; yes, I'm beginning to see the bottom of the stream, even from where I am resting on Mama's back.

Mother, who has so far been in good spirits, going about her task with enthusiasm, all of a sudden appears low-spirited.

"What is wrong with you, Mama?" That was Kwaku, my big brother. He likes to make a show of possessing the gift of reading minds.

"I am disappointed."

"Why?"

"It appears luck is not on our side today. I'm looking at the very bottom of the stream. It appears apart from a few eels as well as a small number of tilapia and herrings, nothing else dwells here! The notion of having expended so much energy to drain a long section of the stream only to be met with such a meagre catch is driving me crazy!"

"That is the punishment for trying to reap where you have not planted!"

"Shut up, you insolent boy! Stop adding salt to my injury, or I'll give you a slap on the face!"

"I have an idea how to avoid a similar situation in the future."

"What idea?"

"We should consider growing our own fish!

"Growing our own fish? How can that be?"

"One of my playmates told me his father taught him it is possible to rear fish at home, just in the same way we rear fowl, goats, sheep, etc."

"That is strange news to me!"

"Well, that is what my friend told me."

"What is his name?"

"Yaw Manu."

"Is he not Kofi Aworo's second child?"

"Yes indeed."

"So he heard it from his father Kofi Aworo?"

"Yes, Mama."

"Um! Don't believe everything that comes from Kofi Aworo! He is well known in the village for the tendency to exaggerate as well as spreading wild rumours and stories!"

*

We are on our way home. As Mother had anticipated, it wasn't a good catch. Poor Mother! After spending hours draining the stream with me stuck to her back for most of the time, she ended up catching almost nothing!

1T

A HORROR ROUND TRIP

I really do hope I will never ever have to endure the hassle I am about to report. Two days ago, that is a day before yesterday, in the evening, one of our relatives came to announce that one of Mother's cousins had passed away, at Amantia, Mother's place of birth. From my information, Amantia is where she grew up and lived until she met Father. Eventually she accompanied him to our present village, Mpintimpi.

On hearing the sad news Mother wept for most of the evening. I have indeed never seen her so sad and upset. I hear she grew up with her departed cousin. A close bond eventually developed between them.

The next day, that is yesterday, Mother packed her items into a small travelling bag. After breastfeeding me to the full, she put on a predominantly black dress with a black scarf to go with.

"Mama, where are you going?" Kwame inquired.

"To Amantia."

"But it is not Christmas yet?"

"What gave you that idea?"

"I thought we would only visit there during Christmas!"

"Well, Christmas is still far off; nevertheless, I am on my way there."

"Okay, I shall also get dressed."

"No, you are not coming along."

"Why not?"

"This is not a pleasure trip, my dear little one. I am on my way to bury my dead cousin."

"Who will take care of me?"

"Your Father."

Kwame was not amused and left the scene sobbing.

Soon we were on our way. Mother fastened me to her back. Kwadwo, our relative who was sent on an errand to break the news, helped her carry her bag. After waiting by the roadside for quite a while, a vehicle finally drove by. As usual, the vehicle was full and I could hardly get air to breathe. The progress was slow. The vehicle stopped at almost every village to allow others to get down or climb onto it. The driver had just driven off again when it stopped, struggling to move on. It could hardly move on.

"What's going on?"

Soon it became clear—the vehicle had sustained a puncture. I could read the anxiety in the face of Mother who understandably was in a hurry to get to her destination to pay her last respects to her departed cousin prior to his burial.

After a while I became restless and began screaming—I was not the only baby on board. Did my scream infect them? I cannot say for sure. What is indisputable is that a couple of other children began crying as well shortly after I had begun crying. Was it because of the disturbing noises of the babies, was it due to the heat in the packed vehicle? Well, many of the young and agile young men and women on the vehicle climbed down from the congested vehicle and into the fresh air. After about twenty minutes, the driver and his assistant managed to change the punctured tyre. Soon we resumed our journey.

About twenty minutes after the resumption of our journey along the rugged, pothole-infested road, the vehicle came to an abrupt stop once more.

"What is the matter?" Many passengers directed their questions at the driver and his mate.

"I have no idea. Please bear with me as I make my first assessment," the driver said.

Together with his mate they went to examine the engine. After about five minutes they reported their findings in the hearing of everyone:

"Sorry, we are out of fuel!"

"That cannot be true! Don't you have a fuel gauge?" the impatient passengers inquired, their exasperation clearly written on their faces.

"Sorry, the gauge is not functioning. I filled my tank fully before setting out. Based on my experience, I reckoned it would take us to the next town where there is a filling station. Unfortunately, that is not the case."

"So what is the way forward?" a passenger sitting just in front of Mama inquired.

"There is a petrol filling station about three miles ahead of us. I am dispatching my two mates with plastic jerry cans. They are very fast walkers, so they should be back in no time. I am even hoping a vehicle will pass by so they can hitchhike and return even more quickly."

As we waited, I could read the frustration in Mother's face. After waiting for a good while, the assistants returned and we were able to resume our journey. After travelling about an hour along the bumpy road, the vehicle came to a stop in the middle of a town which appeared several times bigger than our little village. Mother and her relative got down.

"Thank goodness the ordeal of travelling in that congested vehicle is over!" she sighed.

Initially, I thought that was our final destination—but no, that was not the case! From what I learnt from Mama's conversation with our relative, our destination was a further seven miles away. A smaller road branching from the one we had been travelling on led to the place.

"It is too late to carry on with the journey!" Mother said. "We have a relationship here. We can go and spend the night there."

Well, I thought they might not be happy to receive such unannounced visitors, but that was not the case. Indeed, contrary to my expectations, we were very well received.

We left our very hospitable relations early in the morning to continue on the last leg of our journey.

"Let us hurry up, Kwadwo, to get there in time for the burial. He was a relation dear to my heart and I want to bid him a personal farewell."

Though the road we travelled on from Mpintimpi was not the best of roads, the branch road leading to our final destination was nowhere near it in comparison. It was in a very poor state, made worse by recent rains. We had only travelled a short distance when the vehicle got stuck in mud.

The men travelling on it, about half a dozen of them, tried to use their manual strength to free it from the no-go situation—to no avail.

"Please be patient. I am sending my assistant to the next village to look for a tractor to help pull us out of the sludge," the driver announced to the disappointed travellers.

The assistant returned after a while with no good news to report. "There is indeed a tractor in the village but it has broken down. The owner has sent his assistant to Akim Oda, the district capital, to look for a mechanic who can repair it."

In the end we had to make the rest of the journey on foot. Unfortunately, at the time of arrival the departed relative had already been buried. For the rest of the day Mother was inconsolable. How do I know? Well, she kept wailing for the rest of the day. I must say that it wasn't Mother alone who went about wailing. No, almost everyone I came across was doing the same. It appears it is the culture of my tribe to wail loud for their dead. I just wonder if I will be called upon to do likewise when I grow up.

*

We are on our way back home. Mama spent three days in the village of her birth. The vehicle we are travelling back in is as usual packed to the last seat. I think in future I will stop mentioning this to avoid unnecessary repetition, since it happens to be part and parcel of the transportation system in our area—if not the whole country.

There's one happy note to sound though—the road has dried up, so not as muddy as it was the other day.

We have in the meantime been in the vehicle for a considerable while. Judging from the time we have already spent in the vehicle, we should be nearing home.

I am not the only baby in the crowded vehicle. The adults are patient with us—they do not seem to be bothered by the constant yelling and crying of a baby or toddler. This has been going on all the time.

Oh, did I say only the babies and toddlers are loud? Ach, a couple of the adults are as well. Some of them seem unable to keep their mouths shut and have been conversing quite loudly all along!

*

I might have slept for a short while. I have been awakened by shouts and screams of "Jesus, Jesus!" mingled with yells of *Agyeeii, Agyeee, Agyeeeii!*" My goodness, what is going on here? There is really something amiss here. Not only Mama, but everyone else is screaming at the top of their voices. All pandemonium seems to have broken loose!

The light in the vehicle has darkened; I can smell smoke, I am unable to breathe properly. Oh, I can see red! Yes, I can see flames—coming from the front of the vehicle. The vehicle is on fire! Am I going to be burnt to ashes?

Mother has me firmly in her grip; she is struggling to get out of here. She has managed to push to the edge of the seat. The ground is about a metre and a half below. Is she going to throw me onto the bare ground?

Oops! I am flying in the air. Someone, please catch me! Thank goodness a gentleman who has already managed to jump out has caught me mid-air. So I am safe. What about my dear Mum? Oh, she is struggling to climb down. It appears her clothes are stuck in the wooden frame of the vehicle.

Hurry up, dear Mother, get out of the danger zone! Oh, my heart is racing; I hope I can stop it—but I am helpless. Is it in reaction to the tension that has built up in me?—it might well be the case!

Oh, thank goodness, Mother has managed to climb down from the vehicle. Thank goodness, she is now out of danger—so is almost everyone—with the exception of two young men. They are really kind-hearted. They intentionally stayed back so as to help the others out of danger. Now that everyone is safely on the ground the two gentlemen have also left the vehicle. The fire has so far been confined to the engine compartment. It was the smoke that appeared to be causing much of the problem.

The driver, his assistant and some of the passengers, are frantically trying to put out the flames. So I am in the safe hands of Mother. We have come out of the danger unscathed. Mother has also managed to rescue her luggage. The fire now appears to be under control, though there is considerable smoke billowing from the vehicle into the skies.

How far are we from home? How do we get there? These are nagging unanswered questions in my mind.

"Let's continue our journey on foot," one of the passengers suggests. "There is no point waiting. In the first place the road is sparsely frequented by vehicles. Apart from that any passenger vehicle that passes may already be full."

"I will come along!" Mother says, joining in the discussion. "Mpintimpi is barely three miles away. With her long-term memory, my grandmother used to tell me when she was growing up, there were hardly any vehicles in the country. They did all their journeys, even travels that sometimes covered considerable distances, on foot. So please, someone, please help get the load on my head!"

One of the young men I just referred to has responded to her request and is helping her lift the load from the ground onto her head. So, we are on our way home. The unmerciful sun blazes down on us, for it is midday and it is scorching hot.

*

I might have fallen asleep. I am awake now—in a familiar environment. Kwame and Kwaku are kicking a green orange fruit in an open area between our home and the bush. They seem to be enjoying a game of football—or should I rather say a game of *orangeball*!

So, at last the horror trip to Mother's village has come to an end. I really hope there won't be a repetition of the terrible ordeal anytime soon.

1U

A TORTOISE EVENT

Mother the busy bee is on her feet again! I am fastened to her back. She is preparing a meal of fufu.

I will not dwell on Mama's routine of preparing a meal of fufu, for I don't want to bore the reader with repetition. But this occasion is something special, at least in regard to the soup that will go with the fufu balls.

Father returned from the woods with a strange animal. When I saw it for the first time, I thought it was a small wooden box. To my astonishment, however, it began moving around! For a moment it slipped my mind that no one in the home could understand me! So turning to Kwaku who happened to be standing near where I was lying, I inquired: "Hey Kwaku, is that a living creature?" Of course, no answer was forthcoming.

From the conversation that has been going on between the members of the family, the strange creature is known as a tortoise. Mother will soon begin to prepare a soup of tortoise to go with the fufu balls!

During the exchanges, I heard Mother state that tortoise meat does not taste good if cooked in a thin soup, that is, a soup obtained from mixing ground pepper and tomatoes. Instead, according to her, tortoise meat is best cooked in peanut butter soup or in soup obtained from the flesh of the palm fruit.

On this occasion, it is being prepared with palm soup. I want to explain briefly how palm nut soup is prepared. To begin with, the palm fruit is boiled for about fifteen minutes. The boiled fruit is then pounded in a wooden mortar for a while. The aim of the pounding, I understand, is to free the freshy covering from the nut enclosed within the fruit. On this occasion, Kwabena, who happens to be on holiday, has been assigned the task. He doesn't look amused, though he is carrying out the task dutifully.

After pounding the boiled palm fruit for a while, the whole mixture has been poured into an aluminium bowl. Mother has poured about two litres of lukewarm water into the mixture and is stirring it with her bare right hand. After stirring for a short while, she has poured the whole of the contents into a sieve placed on an aluminium cooking dish. An orange to red coloured liquid or fluid has collected in the dish. Mother now pours away the nuts and fibre that remain on the sieve.

Mother has finally poured the orange to red coloured liquid just referred to over the tortoise meat already simmering in an aluminium soup dish together with onions, pepper and tomatoes. After allowing the soup to boil for a while, Mother removes the cooking dish from the fire. The palm nut soup laced with tortoise flesh is now ready to be served.

After about twenty minutes of pounding, the fufu balls are also ready. So now the long-awaited fufu meal with palm nut soup laced with tortoise meat is ready to be served.

The boys are as usual eating from a common plate. As on several previous occasions, an argument has arisen between them, with the smaller boy accusing his bigger brother of taking more than his fair share; in other words, he is accused of cheating, the argument being about how the meat has been shared amongst the two.

Was it because this time it involves a type of meat considered a delicacy? In any case the heated exchange between the two seems to be getting out of control—to the extent Mother has felt the need to intervene.

"Hey you boys, you have got to learn to tolerate each other."

"It is not my fault! It is Kwame's fault—never satisfied with what he gets!" Kwabena exclaims.

"It is your fault—always trying to keep the better part of everything for yourself!" Kwaku says, siding with Kwame.

"I count on your sense of fairness, Kwabena, to share everything equitably, otherwise I will assume that responsibility myself."

"You just have a look, Mama! Do you recognize any difference between the three portions!" Kwabena shows the plate containing the meat assigned to each of them to Mama.

"Not really," Mother concludes.

"Are you sure, Mama?" Kwame is still protesting.

"No, I did not notice any difference. So you boys, you keep quiet and enjoy your meal and leave me in peace!"

So now some peace seems to prevail in the camp of my brothers.

I am lying on Mother's lap. For now I will keep my peace and allow her to enjoy her meal—well deserved, I should say, considering the effort she has invested so far.

The smell from the soup is intoxicating. I wish I was big enough to take part in the meal! Then I would have teeth to bite into the tortoise meat myself, to enjoy first-hand what appears to be a high-quality meal—at least based on what I am hearing from other members of the family.

1V

CRAWLING WOES

A ch, I am tired of lying on my back all the time and passively observing life around me, day in and day out. Yes, just watching everyone moving around. Of late I have sensed some strength in my limbs. I will try and see whether I can manage to crawl around.

Hey, I have managed to sit without any assistance! The others seem to be excited by my move. I will make a move towards them. Here we go! One, two; one, two. I am moving forward! They are clapping for me! I am spurred on further. So forward, forward, I move!

I am really enjoying it! There is a problem though. The compound is bare earth covered with gravel, and stones, yes stones of all sizes. I can really feel pain and discomfort in my palms and under my knees, my bare knees. It is strange but after crawling for a while the initial pain that I felt has subsided. Has the joy and excitement of being able to move around freely numbed the pain?

*

I am enjoying the new freedom brought about by my ability to crawl freely around. So I have decided to undertake an "expedition" to explore my environment.

Ach! I have spotted a mother hen—from our own stock, I suppose. She is followed by several young chicks. I guess they are only a few days old. Oh, how lovely and cute they appear! They are making *cuck, cuck* noises as they go. Proud mother hen, there she goes, moving gracefully yet majestically along the compound of our home, her little ones following in her trail.

Inquisitive me! I have resolved to follow them—just to have a closer look at the sweet little ones. I am crawling as fast as I can. Well done! I have caught up with them. Two of the little ones noticing my presence have stood still and are staring at me. They are still gazing at me. They are perhaps curious, wondering why only I, among the human population, happens to be going on all fours! Well, if they are so fascinated with me, then I will develop our friendship.

"Hey sweet ones, how are you doing?"

They are still staring at me.

I want to repeat: "Hey sweet ones, how are you doing?"

Apparently they do not understand me, just as in the case of my human compatriots. From the expression on their faces they seem to be enjoying my company though.

Okay, I will pick up one of them if only to have a closer look. I have put my words into action, so I am holding one of them. Oh, it looks so cute! It appears frightened, and is struggling to flee itself. Unable to do so, it has begun crying—or should I say making noises?

"Don't be frightened, sweet little one. I am not out to harm you!"

*

Mother hen has turned to take a look at what is happening to its little ones. She doesn't seem amused. Hey, mother hen is charging toward me!

"Hey, draw back, I mean your little one no harm!" I am trying to reassure her. Mother hen appears unconvinced—still charging towards me! Hey, someone please rescue me from the fury of mother hen, please, someone please hurry! Ouch; that hurts! She has attacked me with her beak. Help, help! I am screaming at the top of my voice.

Whack! Another peck; and yet another! I am yelling and yelling at the very top of my voice!

The sight of blood oozing from my body has sent cold chills down my spine, leading me to yell even louder. At last, my screams have attracted the attention of other members of the family. From all directions they rush to my rescue. Kwame is the first to reach me. He is not big enough to carry me, so he takes hold of both my hands and drags me along the gravel away from my attacker, the gravel causing me additional pain. Finally, Mother has arrived at the scene. She lifts me up, a timely rescue from the "war zone"!

"Be careful little one! Next time don't go near mother hen, okay? They can be aggressive, especially when they are taking their very young ones around. They will indeed go to any length to defend their little ones from danger—real or perceived!"

Ach, that was frightening, really terrifying! How could I imagine my good intentions, yes, my gesture of friendship towards the chicks could be so misinterpreted! For the first time ever, I have seen blood coming from my body! Hope the wound heals quickly without complications!

*

It appears danger lurks everywhere I go. Indeed, hardly had I recovered from the painful confrontation with mother hen, before I was exposed to yet another peril! Maybe Mother should keep me in a cage until I am big enough to lead an independent life! It appears indeed that I require an around the clock protection at this stage of my life.

How can I expect such all-round protection from my parents in view of their busy schedule? And my brothers? They would rightly tell me to the face: "We are not our brother's keeper! We grew up under the same conditions, so you have got to learn to survive under the prevailing conditions. You only have to learn to know your limits!"

Why indeed should my brothers level the accusation of going beyond my limits against me? Does trying to explore one's environment justify such a charge?

On second thought, I think I might as well take the advice of my brothers in view of what I am just about to report. Oh, the daredevil adventurer I am! Realising everyone in the home was busily engaged in some kind of activity, I decided not to remain idle. Instead, I decided to further explore my environment!

Soon I was crawling around. Moments later, I was attracted by the flame coming from the clay stove built in the open compound. Except in case of bad weather when cooking is done in our small clay hut serving as our kitchen, much of the cooking is done on the open stove. On seeing the burning fire, something in me urged me to draw closer and have a look.

Soon I was on my way—not bothered by the discomfort caused to my knees and palms from the rough surface I was crawling over. As I drew closer, I began to feel the heat; never mind! The urge to examine the fire closely overrides anything else!

Meanwhile I had drawn quite close to the fire. Ach, inquisitive me! Instead of leaving it to mere observation, I stretched my hand towards it, with the intention of pulling out a piece of the hot charcoal for closer examination! Even before I could touch the burning coal, the burning sensation was so terrifying it caused me to scream at the top of my voice. My loud scream drew the attention of other members of the family.

"Jesus me!" I could hear one of them scream.

From all directions they rushed to my rescue. This time Kwaku was the first to get to me; quickly, he pulled me out of the danger zone and into safety! It may sound bizarre, but somehow the general commotion caused by the screams of other family members, rather than the burning sensation I felt, was what really frightened me. For a while hell seemed to have descended on our home.

After a period that seemed like eternity to me, calm finally returned to our home.After I had stopped crying and settled down, Mother turned to me to warn me of the danger of fire in future.

"Hey, my dear, don't play with fire—it could burn you!"

Mother did not need to point that out to me, for I had now experienced fire from a close distance and felt the pain in my body. For the next several days, the burning sensation from the encounter lingered on.

1W

A NEAR-SUFFOCATION EXPERIENCE

I am dying, really dying. In fact, I am beginning to give up the fight. The end may well come as a relief—to end the never-ending woes and suffering I have been subjected to since I joined this community several months ago. Yes, indeed, the pain on the left side of my neck has become unbearable! It all began several days ago, with a feeling of discomfort on the affected area of my neck. After a short while it developed into a lump. In time the lump grew larger and larger. At the beginning of my problem, I could still easily swallow; now I can hardly swallow.

The lump is not only hindering my swallowing, it is causing me considerable pain.

Usually, I would scream to draw attention to my pain. Now even crying has become an ordeal; to put it even more bluntly, my voice has disappeared! The excruciating pain, the struggle to swallow, the difficulty in breathing and the inability to even cry—they are all becoming too much for me to bear. Why can't someone just come to my aid! Impossible! Hey, whoever brought me here, can you please do something to bring an end to my woes?

*

This is really strange. I thought it was in the real world. Just as I was contemplating my sorry state, all of a sudden I saw myself standing before a very huge individual! He was so huge he reached from the ground to high, high beyond the skies. He was blocking my way, so I begged him to make way for me to pass him.

"No going forward; get back to where you came from!" came his loud, firm and authoritative voice.

"Please allow me to continue my journey, I am not happy where I am. A huge boil has developed around my neck. The two individuals in charge of me are not doing much to end my suffering."

"No, no, no! You have to fulfil the mission for which you were sent."

"But I cannot bear the suffering!"

"You have to persevere, my little one. All will be well."

"When then?"

"At the right time!"

"Today, tomorrow, the day after tomorrow?"

"I refuse to reveal the exact time, the day and place to you—it won't be long though."

"Please, please, tell me."

"Shut up little one and go back where you came from. At the count of three you will be on your way. One, two…!"

*

Oh, I can hear a sizzling noise—the mosquitoes again! But I thought they come to disturb the human population only at night and not in the middle of the day? Where then is this giant of a person I just spoke to? Was I dreaming, or perhaps daydreaming? Ach, everything appears confusing, really confusing.

*

I have been counting the days when I first noticed the change to the left side of my neck. If I am right in my counting, then today is the fourteenth day. Now at last Papa and Mama have decided to seek outside help after their various herbal remedies, mixtures and creams have failed to make any difference.

I thought they were heading for the Roman Catholic Hospital at Nkawkaw, to my good friends. Well, from what I have overheard my parents say, the general opinion here is that a boil or an abscess cannot be treated in hospital. Yes, they are saying that conventional medicine has no effect on boils. So they are taking me to a traditional healer at Afosu, which from what I hear is about four miles to the south of our village.

I am wondering why they have so far not contacted Papa Osei? I can only wonder; after all, he is reputed to be very competent in the area of traditional medicine. Never mind; as far as I am concerned, what is important is to get help—whatever help is needed to bring an end to my woes.

*

I am not feeling well at all. Not only the affected area is hurting badly, the pain has spread around my whole neck. Now it has radiated into my head. Ouch, my whole head is aching badly. Previously, I could with considerable effort manage to get some fluids down. Now it appears the whole passage beyond the tongue is blocked! I am not only choking, I am suffocating as well. Today could very well see the end of my journey.

Ouch! Yet another setback! I have just heard Father tell Mother that there is no way they can find a means of transport at this time of the day. They have agreed that they cannot afford to wait another night for fear of losing me. So they have decided to do the journey on foot. Mother is saying that my condition is such that I stand the danger of suffocating should she fasten me to her back. So they have decided to bear me in turn with their outstretched arms. Two other relatives have volunteered to accompany them, to help carry me. I find them very kind.

We are now on our way. We have been walking quite a while. It has turned dark. Papa thought ahead; he took a torchlight along. He has now switched it on, to provide the only source of light in the utter darkness. I thought the moon would be sympathetic and provide light to brighten our way. On this occasion, she has chosen to desert us—never mind.

After walking a period of time which seems eternal to me, we have arrived at the outskirts of what appears to be quite a large town. Mother and the rest of the group have left the road on which we had been travelling. We are now walking on a little street on each side of which are buildings of various sizes. Father has knocked on the gate of a large rect-angular building. After waiting for a while, the gate opens. Beginning with Father, everyone goes through it.

An elderly person, who appears slightly bent at the waist and who is supporting himself with a walking stick, has met us within the courts of the home and offered everyone a seat. After exchanging greetings and conversing for a while, Mother has handed me to the stranger. Under normal circumstances I would be crying and screaming in protest. Well, I feel so weak and frail, I have no energy left to do so.

After the elderly man examines me with a critical eye, he directs his glance at Mama, Papa and the other two individuals I referred to earlier on.

"Serious, very serious!" he says. "You should have brought him ear-lier. Of course, this is no time to apportion blame. I will do what I can and leave the rest to the One up there." With that he points to the skies.

"Thank you very much for your help," Mother says. "I really do hope you are able to help." I can see the tears flowing from her eyes.

"It is now too late to prepare the medicinal concoction," the old man says. "Go and rest for the night and return early tomorrow. If he is able to make it through the night, he will surely make it."

*

It is early the next morning. We are back at the home of the tradi-tional healer.

"Wait a minute while I go to the woods to collect the necessary ingredients," he instructed my parents.

The stranger is back after being away for a while. He has instructed an assistant to pound the ingredients he collected from the woods in a stone crucible, into a paste. His instructions are dutifully followed. The assistant places the paste into a bowl and hands it to the healer who applies the paste directly on the boil and its surroundings. Ouch! The paste has a cooling effect on the affected area, though. I can only hope it leads to an improvement.

A while has passed since the cream was applied but I'm feeling even worse than before. I can hardly breathe—the battle seems to be going badly against me.

*

I might have dozed off but I'm awake now. I can sense a lot of activity going on around me. It appears the sounds and noises resulting from the frenetic activity awakened me from sleep. Mother, Father, the strange man and his assistant—they all appear to have their hands full of activity. What's going on? I can feel fluid flowing from the side of my neck where the boil was; it appears I am losing a substantial amount of fluid from that side of my neck!

*

Ach, that's scary! Mother has just removed a piece of towel completely soaked with dark red blood. Did all that blood come from my little body? I'm afraid I'm going to lose all the fluid in my body!

But the good thing is that since the boil burst to release fluid, my breathing has improved. Whereas before that I had the impression of being choked to death, now I can breathe quite easily. Thank goodness, the constant pressure on my neck has also eased considerably!

The stranger, I mean the medicine man, has just entered the room. He has turned to Mother, a broad smile on his face:

"Thank God, the boil has burst! Your little one will live!" he announced reassuringly.

"We are grateful for your help!" Mother smiles. "When we first got here I had all but given up hope. Indeed, I had almost resigned myself to the thought of losing him. Now I can see a ray of hope on the horizon."

She thought she was going to lose me?! Did I hear Mother right? Lose me to whom? I just don't understand what that means. Was she concerned someone was going to snatch me and take me away? If so, then who does she mean and where was that individual going to take me to?

As I have stated on not a few occasions, though I can understand them, I don't always get the real sense of what is behind the spoken words. But never mind! What is important to me is that the pressure on my neck has eased considerably, enabling me to breathe quite easily and without the need to strain myself.

*

I thought we would be heading straight back home now. That doesn't appear to be the case, judging from the fact Mother is not showing any sign that we are about to leave. But now I've got the confirmation. Papa has told Mama we need to stay overnight for the sake of precaution. Since the road we will travel on is in a bad shape, they are concerned that the shaking and bumping of the vehicle we will be travelling on might cause me unbearable pain. Papa and Mama are very caring parents indeed!

*

The next day has dawned. We are back home. The homeward journey was, as feared, quite bumpy. I breathed a sigh of relief when it was all over.

*

Several days have elapsed since the boil on my neck burst. The wound has healed completely. Apart from some discomfort that I experience from time to time over the scar, everything is fine with me.

YEAR 2

2A

A BIRTHDAY PARTY THAT NEVER WAS

From my own calculation, today marks my first birthday!
    Hello, why is no one congratulating me on my special day?
"Hey, Papa, Mama, Kwame and Kwaku, has the idea not occurred to
any of you to congratulate me and also to sing me a 'Happy birthday to
you' song?" I am trying in my own way to draw the attention of other
members of the family to the matter, making use of the little Twi that I
think I know. So, I am producing sounds which as far as I am concerned
stand for: "Hey why are you not congratulating me on my birthday?"

To my dismay, no one seems to understand me! My brothers even
find what I am doing funny.

"Hey Mama," Kwame calls out to Mother, "just come over and listen to your *prince*! He is making funny noises—'puh puh; buh buh; bah,
bah!' I don't know what he is up to!"

I am really disappointed. Or is celebrating birthdays not part of the
culture here? It can possibly be the case. Indeed, since my arrival here
I have never heard anyone talking about celebrating a birthday. Surely,
the respective birthdays of other members of the family have come and
gone during the course of the year! Well, if no one is wishing me a
happy birthday, I can wish myself the same. So I am singing the "Happy
Birthday To You" song to myself!

*

Hey, the "Happy Birthday To You" song seems to have attracted other members of the community, I mean the four-legged beings roaming around! Do they perhaps sense that today is my special day? Or is it mere coincidence? In any case, about half a dozen of them have gathered around me! A couple of them are staring intently at my face. Are they perhaps bidding me a happy birthday—doing what the others have failed to do?

*

I have been breastfed. Mother allowed me a bit more time to fill my tummy with breastmilk. Was it perhaps a special treat to mark my special day? Mother caring about such matters? I really have my doubts.

*

The rest of the family are enjoying their breakfast—the same boiled plantain and *kontomire* sauce. It has just occurred to me that I hardly find any meat or fish in the sauce. It is definitely not intentional, not because any of them dislike meat or fish. No, that is not the case, for whenever Father manages to hunt a prey, everyone seizes the opportunity to consume as much of the meat as they can get. I think it boils down to the matter of cash—which always appears to be in short supply here.

*

It can't be true! They are taking me to the farm on my birthday!! But what choice do I have? So, whether I like it or not, I am fastened once again to the back of Mother, accompanying her to the farm.

Kwame and Kwaku, as usual, are walking ahead of Mother. In this respect I am more privileged; the thought of a time in the near future when I will also have to walk barefooted to the farm is daunting to put it mildly.

We have arrived on one of our farms. From the conversation going on, it is the plot of land cultivated in the previous years. The young cocoa plants have to be freed of the bushy undergrowth encroaching on them and threatening to kill them! In other words, the bush has to be weeded away. That is exactly what Father is doing. He has hired the services of a casual labourer to assist him. I hear they are also called "By days"—because they are paid on a daily basis. Mother will first cook lunch for them and later join in the assignment already referred to.

I am still fastened to her back. The air is refreshing. The sun is in the blue sky, but it's not very hot yet; it will surely be much hotter in the course of the day. There are some birds singing too. I hear some croaking sounds of frogs coming from the woods, not far from where we are. I was frightened by them during my early days on earth—no more!

I can observe Father at work. He is bent slightly forward. Armed with a machete, he is weeding the undergrowth, to prevent them from encroaching upon the crops growing on the land. The casual labourer is working alongside him. The stranger, who looks to be many years Father's junior, appears to be bubbling with considerable energy. He is clearing the bush at a really quick pace, leaving Father far, far behind!

*

I might have fallen asleep. Now I am awake—or better still, half-awake. I can hear loud screams and shouts all around me. Amid the cacophony of noises, I can make one word out—*snake*: "Snake, snake, snake!" Everyone is crying out. Snake? What in the world does the word stand for?

"Wow!" Someone has just lifted me up! The stranger I just referred to ran quickly to where I was lying, picked me up and carried me away as quickly as he could.

Out of the cacophony of noises, I can make out Mother's voice.

"Kwaku, why did you leave him alone?" she is screaming at my brother.

"I left him for a short while so I could open my bowels!"

"Didn't I tell you to let me know if you needed to leave your position so I can come to relieve you?"

"Yes, you did!"

"Why then didn't you keep to the instructions!"

"Sorry Mum!"

"Now I hope you realize what happened! The dangerous cobra could have bitten and killed him with its poisonous venom!"

Being attacked by a cobra! Oh, what a lucky escape! How did I get myself into such a dangerous situation? Well, based on the conversation that transpired among family members, this is what happened: I fell asleep whilst I was fastened to Mother's back. To give her a freer hand to go about her activities, she decided to, as it were, put me to bed on the field. She created a makeshift sleeping place making use of the broad leaves of a banana plant growing on the field.

After putting me to 'bed', she placed me in the care of Kwame, with the instruction never to leave me alone. He was to notify Mother if he needed to vacate his position, for her to send a replacement before leaving. As it turned out, Kwame did not keep to the instructions and left me alone to obey the call of nature, without informing Mother.

As it turned out, not long after he had left me alone, a green cobra was crawling past and, out of curiosity perhaps, drew closer to cast a glance at the little human being lying alone in the woods! Just as it drew very close to me, Kwame, returning from his adventures in the bush, spotted the snake and began screaming at the top of his voice: "Snake, snake!" The shouts drew the attention of the others who rushed to my rescue. The visiting crawling being, apparently taken aback by the commotion, quickly fled the scene. What a bizarre, indeed remarkable, event to coincide with my very first birthday!

2B

THE FIRST STEPS THAT WENT AWRY

I am really envious of other members of the family. Whereas they are able to move about—walk, run, jump, hop, etc—at will, what I can show in return is merely crawl around!

Over the last several days I have become increasingly aware of bursts of energy in my legs. On such occasions, a voice in me seems to tell me to "get up and walk!" Is it out of fear? Is it because of being overcautious? I cannot say for sure, but the fact remains that I have so far suppressed that urge, as it were, to venture into the unknown.

No more! I have resolved that should I feel a burst of energy as I crawl around, I will seize the opportunity and venture onto my feet—come what may!

I am crawling around. The other members of the family are pounding—guess what?—fufu! It appears the world of our home will cease to exist the day the rhythmic sound of fufu remains silent.

I am still crawling around. I have spotted a green bunch of leaves. I will crawl over and have a closer look; to satisfy my curiosity. One of our *Baa-Baa-baa*s has just grabbed it just as I was about to get hold of it. No, I won't let this insolent fellow go unpunished! I am crawling at a good speed behind it. Is it because of the excitement? No idea. The fact is, I am beginning to feel a burst of energy in both legs!

"Get up and go chase the *baa, baa, baa*!" a voice is urging me. This time I have decided to act on the advice of the voice.

Wow!! I am on my legs now. Hey, amazing, I can stand on my own! My legs are still a little wobbly and I decide to wait awhile for them to steady before moving forward.

No, I cannot wait for long, or I won't be able to catch the offender. So I am moving forward. Hey everyone, look at me, I am able to walk! I am in pursuit of the naughty fellow, the insolent *baa, baa!*

Aargh, I have lost balance and fallen over! My head has hit the bare ground. Ouch, my head has been shaken violently! Hopefully I have not cracked a bone!

I am screaming loudly! My screams have drawn the attention of other members of the family to my plight! Mother has literally cata-pulted herself from her seat to my aid. She has picked me up and tries to comfort me.

"You have got to exercise some patience, you daredevil!" she smiles. "Your overexuberance will lead you nowhere but into troubles such as this!"

I will take Mother's advice and exercise caution in the way I go about my life in future.

*

I am making good progress in my walking endeavours. I am able to stand upright on my own and move several steps forward without sup-port. Some may call it toddling, not walking in the real senses. I am not bothered by the semantics. What matters to me is my ability to go quite a good distance without support. I am really delighted concerning the opportunity to move around, just like anyone else. Ah! What a glorious feeling, the realization that I no longer need to beg my brothers to do me this and that favour!

There is a downside though! I am forced to walk bare-footed, with-out any protection for the soles of my feet. I am trying to communicate with my parents the need to provide me with at least a pair of socks to shield my soft and tender soles from direct contact with the ground. For reasons I do not want to repeat, that is not possible. Even assuming I am able to communicate with them, I doubt if they would agree to my request. Why? The answer is this: since I joined this community, I have never seen anyone—babies, children, teenagers—wearing any type of footwear, be it socks, sandals, shoes or whatever!

They are likely to shake their heads in disbelief at such expectations from the youngest member of the group. Things may be bearable if the whole compound of our home was cemented or boasted concrete block paving. But no, it is bare earth! It is not earth covered with sand, but rather with stones and gravel. So, I am forced to walk barefoot on stones and gravel—which can be painful indeed.

As if that was not enough, the earth usually turns really hot during the day—the effect of the scorching sun. Walking on the ground with unprotected feet makes the soles feel as if on fire. Despite these challenges, I still cherish my new-found freedom—the freedom to move about freely, without hindrance as I explore my environment.

2C

A HAIRBREADTH'S ESCAPE

Today I had a really lucky escape! What happened, one may ask? Well, there are two coconut trees on the compound of our home. Kwame climbed one of them to pick the ripened nuts. The warning went out for everyone to keep a safe distance. Initially I complied. As I fixed my gaze on my brother near the top of the tree, I soon heard *"buum, buum, buum!"* sounds. I turned to have a look. A pair of nuts that had fallen not far from the tree caught my attention. Out of excitement mingled with a great deal of curiosity, I toddled towards the nut closest to me to examine it closely, disregarding the warning to stay far away from the immediate neighbourhood.

"Hey, boy, don't get too close!" Kwame cried out

"Get away from there!" Mother joined my little brother.

No, I wouldn't listen! Instead, I continued to run towards the harvested coconuts. Just then I heard the sound of *buum, buum,* as another couple of coconuts fell one after the other just near me, one of them missing my head by only a hairbreadth. Moments later, Mama was on the spot to whisk me out of the danger zone. Notwithstanding the stir caused by my reckless behaviour, I soon settled down to enjoy my first ever opportunity to taste cool, refreshing coconut water.

*

2D

TASTY BREASTMILK'S MONOPOLY UNDER THREAT

Today, for the first time since my arrival on earth, Mother is about to offer me a meal to supplement her delicious breast milk. I thought as well that it was indeed high time such a step was taken. I have indeed over the last several days been experiencing hunger pangs. Whether it is because I am growing in size or because Mother's breasts are not producing enough milk to stave my hunger, I cannot say. I hope the additional meal is as tasty as the milk I have been used to so far.

At the moment Mother is in the process of preparing what the others are referring to as *koko*. From the conversation that has been going on between Mother and other members of the family, *koko* can be regarded as porridge prepared from corn meal that has been mixed in water and has been left alone for a couple of days to undergo fermentation. Since this is the first time I am observing Mama prepare the cornmeal porridge, I am going to engage in what can be regarded as a running commentary.

As a first step, Mother has taken a portion of fermented corn meal from a big plastic container half filled with the stuff. Next, a portion of the meal has been placed in a cooking dish half-filled with water. With the help of her right hand, Mother stirs the meal. After stirring it for a while the meal is completely dissolved in the water. Mother has now placed a cooking dish with its contents on the open fire. She is now stirring the mixture on the fire with a ladle.

Kwame has just arrived at the scene—God only knows where from! He has taken note of what is cooking on the fire. That has aroused absolute excitement in my big brother.

"*Koko*! *Koko*! I am delighted at the opportunity to enjoy a portion of *koko*!" he screams at the top of his voice.

"It is too early to rejoice, my dear!"

"Why?"

"It is not meant for you!"

"Not for *me*? Who then?"

"For your little brother. I will cook a meal of *ampesi* for you as usual!"

"No, I will like *koko* as well!"

"There is not enough to go round. Your teeth are strong enough to chew boiled plantains; he can only drink milk and *koko*!"

Kwame, pity him! He appears clearly disappointed—he has burst into tears. He is crying really loud; I've never seen him so upset.

"Enough of your loud crying! Just fetch a bowl from the kitchen."

Kwame is so excited he is running as quickly as he can. He returns with a large bowl in his hands.

"What should I do with that?" Mother asks.

"You asked me to fetch a bowl!"

"Not such a big bowl; just go back and collect a smaller one. You remember the one you used for the rice water the other day, don't you?"

"Yes."

"Hurry, go fetch it."

Is it the joy of expectation that has imbued him with such energy? My little brother dashed into the kitchen and returned in no time, a small plastic bowl in his hand.

Mother pours a ladle filled to overflowing with *koko* porridge into the bowl in Kwame's hands. Instead of leaving the scene, Kwame is still standing near Mother. What is he up to? Expecting more perhaps?

"What are you waiting for?" Mother has turned to him.

"Can you please add some more?"

"More of what?"

"More, *koko*, please!"

"You've got to be satisfied with what you have!"

"Please, only a little more!"

Mother dips the spoon into the porridge one more time. This time the ladle is filled just to about half its volume with porridge. Mother has added it to what is already in Kwame's bowl. He now appears happy, and is walking away.

"Allow some time for it to cool before eating it, okay!"

"No worries, Mama, it will cool down in my mouth!"

"Don't call for assistance when you get your tongue burnt!"

"No, I won't!"

*

Mother has now turned her attention to me. She has poured a little portion of the *koko* onto a small plate. For a while I am just lying on her laps—nothing is happening. She is perhaps allowing it some time to cool. At last, she takes hold of a small plastic spoon and dips it into the porridge and then puts it near my mouth.

"Open your mouth little one." Is she talking to me? How does she know I can understand her language? I am showing nil reaction.

"Hey my dear little one, you open your mouth!"

Still no reaction. Mother's milk or nothing else, I am telling myself.

"Hey boy, hurry up, I have no time to spare—I still have several household chores to perform!"

I'm still not impressed.

Mother's patience appears to have come to an end. With the help of two fingers of her left hand, she exerts gentle pressure on both cheeks. The tactic—or is it a trick? —has worked. Much as I resisted it, my mouth has been forced open. Now a spoonful of porridge has been forced down my throat!

Ach, what a horrible taste; no comparison to tasty breast milk! I am thinking I am being fed acid rather than food! I won't accept it without any resistance though. So I am kicking my legs around and punching both fists into the air. Something is urging me to aim the fists at Mama!

No, that will be going too far. I don't want to show any degree of aggression towards her. She, without doubt, has my interest at heart. But Mother appears unimpressed by my antics. Having already brought up four boys, she must without doubt be used to such childish behaviour. I guess her goal is to get as much of the stuff into my tummy as possible in the shortest possible time; so in quick succession, she forcefully spoon-feeds me two more helpings of porridge. She might have continued for a while—indefinitely perhaps—but for the fact that I am now retching. Yes indeed, I have the feeling whatever has gone down my throat wants to come back!

So Mother has stopped feeding me; she managed to get every bit of the *koko* into my tummy though! In fact, my tummy appears quite distended. After all that resistance I feel short of breath; indeed, my breathing appears laboured. So my first encounter with any type of meal other than delicious breast milk is over. I can only guess what other types of meals I might be fed in the coming days in addition to this awful tasting *koko!*

*

I want to report on yet another 'first' in my life. It happened only a few minutes ago. Mama was as usual enjoying a meal of fufu. I was on her lap. I was settled. That is not always the case. Though unintentional, on not a few occasions I have not left her in peace to enjoy her meal. It may well be that I felt the urge to open my bowels or to empty my bladder, or both, just at the very moment when she was enjoying her meal! On other occasions, my tummy underwent painful spasms or cramps as I was lying on her lap, which in turn forced me to scream for help.

Thank goodness, on this occasion I was fine and settled. As I watched her eating the fufu meal, which as I previously mentioned involves "cutting" chunks of fufu balls, dipping them into soup and swallowing, she cut an unusually small piece of the ball, dipped it into the soup and instead of putting it into her own mouth, turned to me saying: "Open your mouth."

Surprised by this unexpected development I turned and looked away.

"Open your mouth my little one; and try swallowing down this small chunk of fufu."

I kept looking away.

"It tastes good, my dear, so try it!"

At that juncture my recent unsuccessful attempt to resist being fed *koko* flashed through my mind. Not prepared to undergo a repetition, I did as requested. Mother then placed the tiny chunk of fufu on my tongue. For a moment I was reluctant to swallow it.

"Swallow it down, it tastes good!"

I did as requested. Soon the tiny fufu chunk slipped down my throat and into my belly. Though I was not keen on swallowing any additional fufu, Mother used her power of persuasion to get me to swallow down a few additional chunks.

I found the soup that was served with the fufu too spicy for my liking. Indeed, long after I was done with the meal the burning sensation lingered on my tongue.

2E

HACKING COUGH GONE HERBAL

I have been unwell for a while. This time it is mainly coughing. I have been coughing a lot—for most of the day, I must say.

Nightfall has arrived. I am in bed now. The cough is persisting. I can hardly sleep. I am keeping the two adults in the room awake as well. I pity them really, but… well, it is their own fault they haven't got me my own room. In that case, they could have taken turns to look after me. That would allow each of them some time to rest. They might say to my face that it is easier said than done, considering the meagre resources at their disposal. Well then, we are all in it together! I didn't beg them to accept me into their home in the first place!

Back to the terrible coughing attacks—I heard Father tell Mother this type is not an ordinary cough, but rather *nkonkon*. *Nkonkon*? I have never heard about it. I thought the Twi word for cough is *ewa*. Well, Father is saying that *nknoknon* is a cough beyond the ordinary. He went on to say I could go on coughing unceasingly until I collapse and die! Well, if I die, I die!

The usual conversation has been going on between my parents for the last few days—whether to take me to hospital or to try traditional medicine. The obstacle in the way of taking me to hospital is, as in all other instances, money, or the lack of it. Yes, the money issue is playing up again!

"Let's take him to hospital tomorrow," Mother suggests.

"Let's try traditional medicine for a few days," Papa counters.

"I am not against traditional medicine, but I think it is about time to take him to hospital. I am becoming very concerned for his well being.

The cough is not permitting him to be breastfed. The little that gets down is vomited out as a result of the coughing."

"I understand your concern. Let's wait and see what tomorrow brings."

*

Today is Day 7 since the onset of the coughing attacks. Things are getting worse rather than better.

A slender-looking elderly woman arrives. I am seeing her for the first time. She is holding a bottle filled with a red-coloured liquid. She has handed it to Mother. "Try this; it really works wonders. I have tried it in the past on my children presenting similar symptoms—with success in all cases."

Now I am on Mother's lap. Father is also around. A third person, an uncle, Father's younger brother, has also arrived at our compound. He has joined the team. So, I am surrounded by four adults including my parents.

Father has taken hold of my two legs; he is holding both firmly. Uncle on his part is taking care of both hands. Mother is supporting my head tenderly. The strange woman is bending over me, a spoon in her hands. Mother has tilted my head slightly upwards. The stranger has quickly poured a portion of the contents of the bottle into the spoon. I thought she was going to pour the contents into my mouth. But no, she has taken hold of the root of my nose, and poured portions of what was in the spoon into each nostril!

I am feeling a burning sensation in my head. My head feels as if it is on fire, real fire. I cannot find words to describe how I feel!

I thought that was the end of the ordeal, but no! She has now forced my mouth open—and poured a spoonful of the liquid into my mouth! Initially, I kept it in my mouth and wanted to spit it out. But then she read my thoughts! She would not put a happy face for me or waste any more time. Quickly she performed a manoeuvre which involved pressing firmly on the corners of each of my lower jaws. The manoeuvre served its intended purpose and I had no choice but to allow the liquid to run down my throat.

It is superfluous to mention here that I was really disgusted at what I consider her wild, undiplomatic behaviour! As a way of expressing my outrage, I began yelling very loudly. The "iron lady" was not impressed by my protests. Without taking notice of me, she began to address mother:

"Leave him to rest. After he has rested awhile, fill a bucket with lukewarm water, add five big spoons of the mixture to it and stir it for about a minute and bathe him in it. Last but not the least—just before he goes to bed, give him the same amount of liquid as before to drink. The whole procedure should be repeated daily for seven days. He should recover completely at the end of the period."

Whether it is indeed a result of the therapy of the strange woman; or whether it is a case of the problem resolving itself after it has run its course, I cannot say for sure. The fact remains that a little over a week after it all began, I have returned to good health.

2F

RUNNING WITHOUT END

My goodness! My tummy has been running the whole day: I can hardly keep my bowels shut! Mama, pity her! She invests the time and effort to clean me only to be forced by my bowels which seem to be running amuck to repeat the whole procedure once again. Has the running stomach, perhaps, something to do with the change of diet? I am inclined to think that is the case, judging from the fact that at the time when I was being fed exclusively on Mother's milk, I rarely experienced such symptoms

I am not only having frequent stools, I am also vomiting frequently. Is the problem due to the water, the food or both? I just don't know. My reasoning is that the problem will be resolved if I am allowed to return to the practice of feeding exclusively on Mother's milk. Well, it appears that is no longer feasible owing to my increased size, coupled with dwindling milk production on the side of Mother.

Well, if it is no longer possible to return to breastmilk, and the diarrhoea will not stop, then I should preferably be sent to hospital—to my lovely Sisters! Much as I cherish the prospect of meeting my kind friends again, the thought of travelling on one of those trucks with wooden benches sends a cold chill down my spine! Eh! I am having second thoughts about the idea of going to hospital. Much as it will surely be beneficial to me, I am beginning to wonder how somehow discharging watery stools at short intervals can be dealt with while travelling on one of those fully packed vehicles along the rugged, bumpy road! I can only hope things get better so my parents are not forced to make that difficult decision.

*

No, things still don't look good. It is night and still no improvement. I am too young, but it definitely has something to do with the food. It definitely is no coincidence that this problem has cropped up just a few days after I stopped drinking breast milk! It appears indeed that there is something in breastmilk that was preventing me from experiencing the symptoms that have just cropped up. I thought the solution would be simple—just give me breastmilk and end all the unpleasant side effects of eating other food. Well, let's see how things develop in the next several days.

*

Both adults in the room seem to be at the end of their tethers.
"What is the way out of this?" Mother asks.
"The answer is anyone's guess!" Father counters
"Let's seek a loan and take him to hospital."
"Oh, yet another attempt at a loan!" Father sighs. "I am becoming fed up approaching people here for a loan! The experience is degrading, to put it mildly! I have already approached more than one of the few individuals in the community everyone here considers to be well-to-do, at least based on our standards. I spend some time laying bare my personal circumstances. If only such exposure would always be crowned with success! But no! In many instances after I have revealed everything—yes, after I have, as it were, exposed my nakedness before the potential lender, there follows the heart-breaking response: "Sorry, I am not able to help!" That is humiliating, to put it mildly.
"Well, that is a price we have to pay for being poor," Mother says. "Our little boy is losing all the fluid in his body; he is going to dry up and die in the next few days for sure if nothing is undertaken to prevent that happening."
After a short silence, Father resumed speaking. I thought he would be addressing Mother directly; but no, he chose instead to address me!

"Hey you big-headed guy, you better not give us any further head-aches, okay? Your parents are short of cash, so don't put us in further difficulties. You've got to urge whoever brought you to us to heal you tonight!"

Why should Papa choose to vent his anger and frustration on *me*! Referring to me as a big-headed guy; that is not fair of him! I did not elect to visit them! It is his own fault! "Hey, Father, be careful how you talk to me, okay!" Oh, great, he cannot hear me; he will surely hit back with another remark!

Let me consider the matter a bit more seriously. Their nightly conversation almost always revolves around one thing—money! They seem to be in chronic shortage of cash. I just wonder: are they incapable of growing cash on their own, like the way they grow food crops? They could then harvest and spend as much as they wish!

What a pity I am unable to convey my wonderful idea to them. That will be the first message I will pass on to them when I am big enough to talk. But let me pay attention, for Father has resumed talking:

"Okay, let's wait a day or two to see whether the traditional medicine we have been administering begins to show any favourable effects. If that does not happen, we will have no option but to seek a loan to take him to hospital."

*

Is it the herbal medicine that has worked wonders? Or is it my body that has managed to deal with the problem on its own? I cannot say for sure. The fact remains that several days after the problem first began, my stomach has stopped running! I can only hope that this is not just a short spell from an ever-recurring problem that began after I stopped drinking breast milk.

2G

THE TODDLER TURNED HUNTER

Yet another day! We have had our breakfast. It is yet another day of
work on the farm. For the first time ever, I am being asked to *walk*
on my own instead of being carried by either Mama or Papa. As I have
already reported, initially Mother was carrying me on her back. Later,
when I grew bigger and heavier, she stopped doing so. Instead, the duty
fell on Father to carry me on his neck to and from the farm.

Now I am deemed big enough to do the journey on my own—on
bare feet, I might add! So now I am walking in front of my parents,
heading for the woods, for one of our farmlands which is about a mile
away. I really wish I had some shoes on, but no, I have to do without
any, just as in the case of my brothers.

It is early in the morning; the sun is up. Happily, the sun has not
been up long enough to heat the soil. This is likely to change during
the course of the day. Walking barefooted on the heated soil will be like
adding insult to injury.

We have been walking for a while. The soles of my feet have turned
sore and achy. My legs are also beginning to feel heavy and tired. I am
not progressing as quickly as I did at the beginning, leading some members
of the *team* to lose their patience.

"Hey Kofi, hurry up, we cannot spend the whole day on the road!"
one of them says, pointing to me. Please bear with me everyone. Rome,
after all, was not built in a day. Mark it on the wall, everyone—it is
only a matter of time before I will outpace every one of you in walking
tempo!

*

We have just returned home from the field. I did only a portion of the journey on foot. I did indeed put in my best effort. In the end my tempo was too slow for the liking of the other family members.

Father, who was carrying a large piece of firewood, suddenly put it down and concealed it a few metres from the roadside.

"What are you up to?" Kwaku inquired.

"I am hiding it in the woods; I will pick it up at a later date."

"Why?"

"To enable me to carry the little one on my neck; at the pace he is walking, we may not reach home until tomorrow morning!"

Moments later I was seated comfortably on Father's neck. I felt on the top of the world in an elevated position and admired the panoramic view unfolding before my eyes.

*

What an exciting experience I had on the farm today! I have to make an entry before retiring to bed before the details slip my memory. The assignment today involved clearing one of our cocoa farms of the under-growth prior to harvesting the ripened fruits a few weeks later. Mother was as usual there to cook lunch for everyone.

"Give me a machete! I also want to take part!" I requested as the others got to work.

"Big-mouthed Kofi, as usual, always wanting to do what the others are doing!" Kwaku retorted.

"Just have patience, boy," Father said, "a time will come when there will be too much work for you to do! For now, you can just observe us from a safe distance. Don't come too close; you might get hurt!"

I obeyed and kept my distance as instructed.

All of a sudden Kwaku, who was clearing the weeds on a mound on the field, became excited!

"Hey Papa, come and have a look!"

"What?"

"I have seen a hole, a passage leading to the heart of the mound. I can see fresh claw marks which leads me to think it is occupied by a rat—Gambian pouched rat. We've got to get it for dinner today!"

Soon all the others went over to have a look.

"You are right; all indications point to an occupancy by a Gambian pouched rat." On hearing that I attempted to draw closer to have a look.

"Hey Kofi, keep your distance!" Father cried out seeing me approach them.

The noise of the humans gathered on the mound seemed too much for the occupant to bear, for it sprung out of the hole and began running for its life! Incidentally, it headed towards the place where I was standing. The humans together with our two dogs gave chase. As it ran close by me, I sprung after it, trying to catch it with my bare hands! But it was faster than me! As the frightened creature continued to run away, those in pursuit were unrelenting in their bid to hunt it down.

Out of excitement mingled with curiosity, I ran after them as fast as my legs could carry me. Just as one of the dogs which was closest to its heels made a dash forward in an attempt to grasp it by the neck, the pursued creature managed at the very last minute to make a leap forward towards a nearby tree. Moments later it was ascending the tree at a remarkable speed.

On reaching the very top of the tree it rested in one of the branches. As it reclined at the top of the tree, I observed it as it cast a look at its human pursuers and their two dogs below. Though it appeared quite tiny from its safe refuge at the top of the tree, I interpreted the gestures it was making with its head and hands towards its human pursuers as taunts, challenging them to climb up and catch it if they dared!

"Papa, what about cutting down the tree!" Kwaku suggested.

"Cut down this big tree? No, that would be too much work. Beside the work involved, I have intentionally kept it standing on the field to provide shade for the young cocoa trees when growing on the field."

Feeling helpless to intervene in the situation, Father instructed everyone to return to their positions. As they did so, Father all of a sudden turned to 'Poor No Friend', the dog that came closest to catching the prey: "Hey, you good for nothing fellow! You had all the chance in the world to catch the prey, but you blew it!"

Was it the way our usually composed dog reacted to what might be considered a false accusation on the part of its master? *"Wow, wow, who!"* he sent out a series of loud barks directed at his accusers!

2H

BLESS MAMA INDEFATIGABLE

The sky is covered by dark clouds. Mother says it is going to rain and that we need to rush home!

"Everyone get ready," Mother announces, "we have to hurry home. I'll quickly harvest some food—plantain, yams, cassava."

Mother gets the job done quickly. In no time she has packed the foodstuffs onto an aluminium tray. The tray is packed to the high heavens with harvested foodstuffs. Father helps to lift the load from the ground onto her head. He is staying behind, despite the sign of rain. He just announced he still needed to clear a sizable portion of the farmland from the bushy undergrowth before calling it a day.

So we are on our way home. Kwaku and Kwame, as usual, walk ahead. I am behind them, just ahead of Mother. We have gone only a short distance when it begins to rain.

"Keep going, boys, it is just a drizzle," Mother urges us on.

No, it is no longer a drizzle; the heavens have opened up fully! It is no exaggeration—the rain mercilessly buckets down on us.

"Stop boys, let's seek shelter under the big tree just ahead of us!"

"No, I am carrying on, I am not afraid of the rain. You take good care of yourself and your little ones!" That was Kwaku playing the brave boy.

"Me too! I am neither sugar nor salt to fear dissolving." Kwame has sided with his brother.

So off they go, walking briskly away, not the least bothered by the pitiless downpour from the heavens.

"Kofi, be quick, let's seek shelter under the canopy of the trees!" Mother has taken hold of my right hand and is dragging me beside her.

We are now standing under the shade of a big tree, a few metres from the pathway.

Poor Mother, she has to keep on carrying the items on her head as we wait. She might perhaps manage to put it down on the earth on her own, but there is no way she can manage to lift it back up onto her head without assistance! Despite the protection provided by the canopy of the trees, we are still soaked through by the rain. Mother remains calm and composed. She appears indefatigable—a real hero!

The rain has in the meantime subsided considerably. We are now resuming our walk home. I thought the sun would not show up again after the heavy rain, but no, it has! Mother is saying that is a sign the rains will not continue for long. After about half an hour's walk, we are back home. The two boys are safe at home—we are happily united.

21

NTOBURO aka MEASLES ASSAULT

I have on so many occasions reported about myself or someone else at home falling sick. I thought I wouldn't have to do so for a while— but no!

It all began with Kwaku. A few days ago he failed to get out of bed as usual. Mother thought he was pretending, a way of avoiding taking part in the daily morning chores. But that was not the case, for he soon began to throw up. As if that was not enough, he began to shake uncontrollably!

I heard Mother saying something like he has malaria. As on all other occasions when her children were not feeling well, she prepared some mixture and offered it to him to drink. But this time he did not get better and soon some spots began to appear on his body.

"Ach, that looks like *ntoburo*!" Mother remarked on seeing the spots.

"Ntoburo, what is that?" I wondered.

I have in the meantime learnt that *ntoburo* is the Twi word for measles.

"Let's bring him to the attention of Papa Osei; he has a remedy for it," Mama suggested the moment she saw the spots.

*

So we are heading for the home of the "village Doctor" with me stuck to Mama's back. Kwaku is walking slowly ahead. Pity my big brother! He seems indeed to be in a great deal of distress.

After about a five minutes' walk, we entered the main gate of a building. It is a rectangular-shaped building boasting a large inner courtyard.

We are now in the inner courtyard of the building. We have been met by the "Village doctor", a tall, slender elderly man. He appears so slender I can count his bones!

"Oh my goodness, yet another case of measles!" the traditional doctor declares. He seems to be very familiar with the condition for he does not hesitate a minute in coming to the conclusion.

"I thought as much, but was not sure," Mama replies politely. She seems to have great respect for the healer.

"Yes, that is measles for sure! He is not the only one who has caught it. There has been an outbreak in the village. I have already treated several children as well as adults. The last patient I saw left just a few minutes ago."

"Just take a seat and wait as I quickly collect the necessary herbal components from the nearby bush," said he

*

Ach, that was really quick! He barely disappeared from our sight before reappearing! He was carrying a few packs in his hand, which he handed to Mother. He tells Mother what to do. I am paying attention:

"Boil this in about a litre of water. Allow it to cool. Thereafter fill a bottle or any suitable container with it. He is to drink a teaspoonful three times daily." Then he points to another pack in Mother's hands. "This is herbal paste. Apply it three times daily to the body."

"Am I allowed to wash him?" Mother wants to know.

"No, don't wash him with soap for at least a week. You may just dip a towel in water and use it to clean him."

"Thanks for your help. I am very grateful."

"It is a pleasure. I will come over tomorrow morning to check on him."

"Thanks?"

"Any questions?"

"He has not been eating and drinking properly. Can you please give him something for that?"

"No need for any additional medicine, my dear. He is not eating due to loss of appetite caused by the condition. This medicine will uproot the root cause of the problem; thereafter his appetite will return!"

So we ended the consultation and returned home.

*

Two days have elapsed since we visited the village *doctor.* Kwaku is not getting better. Kwame is now also experiencing the same symptoms.

"We are in for trouble!" Mother tells Father. "The prospect of sending both to hospital in case Papa Osei's remedy fails to cure them is disheartening, really disheartening! You Big One up there, be merciful to us!"

"Let's hope for the best. Measles sometimes clears, just the way it came—without leaving any traces."

That is Papa sounding optimistic. What else can he do, judging from his past conversations about the chronic shortage of money in his purse!

*

Hey good friends, is it me developing a kind of disease phobia, or is it real? What is beyond dispute is the fact that I am beginning to feel itchy. My body is indeed itching all over! I will try to be brave and suppress the problem as much as I can so as not to upset my parents. Just imagine how they will feel on realising all their three boys are infected!

*

We have retired to bed. The spirit is willing but the flesh is weak! I have so far tried to suppress the urge to scratch my body in reaction to the intense itching sensation. I can no longer keep resisting! So I am now scratching my body. To my dismay, the more I scratch, the stronger the urge to continue scratching! It is all becoming too much to bear. I have begun to cry.

"What is the matter?"

I cannot express myself. The fact that I am scratching my body has led Mother to suspect the worst.

"Koogyamfi, I suspect the little one has also caught the measles!"

"You don't mean it!"

"Well, he cannot stop scratching. His body is also feeling hot!"

"Misfortunes never come alone!"

"Well, that is what it appears to be."

"Let's wait and see how things develop. I only hope we will not need to take them to hospital!"

After remaining restless for a good while, I was finally overcome by sleep.

*

Kwaku is not eating, Kwame is not eating. I have also lost my appetite—not eating, not drinking!

Here comes Father! He has been on the farm all day long. He is carrying a load on his head. He appears exhausted. He has turned to Mother:

"How are things going?"

"Not, good; not good! We need to act without delay and take them to hospital. I don't want to be scolded by the nurses, the way they did when I turned up late with Kofi's illness!"

"Don't mind the nurses. They seem to be living in a different world! Anyway—for your information I contacted the clerk of the Cocoa Marketing Board on my way here. He is prepared to lend us money against the expected cocoa harvest. Now that the money issue has been settled, we can take them to hospital tomorrow."

"Five of us are traveling to the hospital at the same time! How can that be?" That was Kwaku. After being off food for several days he looks more like a sack of bones rather than the spirited little boy he used to be.

"I understand what you are driving at," Mother says. "You are right; it is not going to be easy, finding five vacant seats on any of the commuter vehicles that pass by—vehicles that in most instances are filled to the last person by the time they reach here."

"In that case," Father says, "I will suggest the following. We will form two groups. In the unlikely event that we find a vehicle which has space for all of us—that is fine. Otherwise, I will travel at the opportunity with Kwaku and Kwame, since their respective conditions are more serious than Kofi's." Which means Mama and the little one will travel at the next opportunity.

*

As planned Father travelled with Kwame and Kwaku at the first opportunity; Mama and I followed a few hours later.

I thought I would see my friends again, but no. That might have been the case if we had slept over. The medical experts however did not consider it necessary to admit any of us, so it turned out to be a day's case.

We were luckier on the return journey—there was space in the vehicle for all of us. So we are all back home. I would be laughing and making jokes about the issue, if it didn't happen to be a serious matter, a matter involving our health and well-being.

What is it about, you might ask? Well, the hospital supplied each one of us with a bottle containing a white-coloured liquid. As I am writing, each one of us has been smeared from head to toe with the white substance. I don't know how best to describe what we have turned to—you might as well describe us as aliens who have returned from a different planet!

But the white liquid seems indeed to be doing wonders, for the itchiness has subsided since the liquid was applied.

I have been concerned that Papa and Mama might catch the disease. I have been told however that both of them caught the condition during childhood so they have nothing to fear since it is highly unlikely one could catch the condition twice! I am only hoping that this is the case, for how can we cope without the support of our parents, in particular Mother's?

2J

STOMACH DISTENSION AND RUMOUR MONGERING

I want to express some important information that came my way today on paper. Over the last several days, I have observed Mother's tummy growing bigger and bigger. Initially I put it down to food, that she has perhaps been eating a bit more of late. Then today, I overheard Kwaku telling Kwame that Mother is expecting a baby.

Kwame was extremely delighted at the news.

"At last, I will share the same fate with that big-headed fellow!" he said, pointing at me. "Mother's favourite that he has become, he will soon have to relinquish that position!" he added.

As might be expected, I was upset by his comments. I decided however not to panic and to approach Mother directly to find out the truth. What I have so far not mentioned is that I have in the meantime been able to speak a few words in the Twi language. Some complain they can hardly understand a word of what I say. Mother is different though—she makes the effort to understand me!

"Mama, Kwame and Kwaku tell me you are carrying a baby in your big tummy. Is that right?" I began.

"Yes, that is the case, my dear," she replied.

"So I am going to get a new brother?"

"Don't talk about a brother; instead, talk about a sister! I am fed up with you boys!"

"So you are carrying a sister?"

"I don't know for sure. I am only praying to the One above to send me a girl!" She pointed to the skies.

"The one above? I cannot see anyone!"

"We cannot see Him with our eyes; but He is there!"

"Can He hear us from there?"

"Not only can He hear us; He can also see us."

"He can see us, though we cannot see Him? Very strange indeed!"

"Well, let us leave Him alone for now and concentrate on our conversation. Yes, I am expecting a baby. I prefer a girl, though I will accept whatever I get."

2K

A RELUCTANT FAREWELL TO
A BELOVED PAL

Does it have anything to do with the conversation I had with Mother yesterday? I can only conjecture. In any case I overheard the following conversation between Mother and Father tonight:

"I will without delay take steps to wean Kofi from breastmilk," Mother said.

"I tell you, that boy won't be amused," Father replied. "The impression I have gained so far is that he is more focussed on breastmilk than those who came before him!"

"Well, I have no choice!" Mother said. "Since this baby in my tummy is due in a matter of weeks, it is imperative I do exactly that—to prevent him competing with the new arrival for breastmilk."

"Do what you consider proper. Even though his loud protests will no doubt cause a few sleepless nights, he has to learn to come to terms with life without breastmilk."

"True!" Mother agreed. "We all had to give up breastfeeding at some point in our lives."

"So when do you intend to begin the weaning process?"

"As early as tomorrow."

So Mother is bent on weaning me off breast milk! The thought of being forced to give up Mother's tasty milk is unsettling to put it mildly. I will definitely not give up easily! The two conspirators involved in the plan should gear themselves up for a real fight!

*

Mother has put her plan into action. For the first time, she is denying me breastmilk!

As planned, I made a decision to protest last night. I won't accept the change without resistance! So, I am putting *my* plan into action. The first weapon I am resorting to is crying. I am not merely crying—I am *yelling* at the top of my voice!

Despite my screams, no one seems to be bothered! What is to be done? Okay, I will add an element of drama to the matter—maybe it will help touch the heart of the main decision maker—Mother! So, I have thrown myself in a dramatic fashion to the bare floor—not without some discomfort, I admit. I am wearing only a slip; my entire upper body is exposed. I am feeling real pain from the stones and gravel pressing on my bare body. I am determined to persevere for a while though. If I am able to achieve a change of heart in my parents, it will be worth the effort.

I am still lying prostrate on the ground and screaming, but it appears no one is paying attention. I have resolved to escalate the matter a bit further—so now I am kicking and also tossing my legs with my hands in the air.

Still no reaction; neither an expression of regret nor a show of sympathy from any member of the family! On the contrary, no one seems to bother.

Meanwhile I am sweating profusely. I can see Kwaku approaching. That is kind of him—at last someone seems to care! He has drawn closer to me and is standing beside me. But his words are shocking:

"Hey you little one, you better shut up and stop disturbing my peace! Do you think you are the only person in this house? If you don't shut up and continue to howl, I will grab you and carry you as far as the perimeter of the compound and leave you there—for good!"

Goodness me, I thought I had found someone to support me! But no! Instead of comfort has come ridicule and rebuke! But I won't allow myself to be intimidated by anyone! Instead of calming down I have become even more agitated, wailing very loudly indeed.

*

I have in the meantime been wailing for almost half an hour. Mother is not impressed and is going about her chores. Kwame and Kwaku are playing football with a green unripe orange they just plucked from an orange tree a few metres away. They seem to be having good fun. I have all along thought oranges are there only to be eaten; well, my brothers seem to have a different opinion on the matter.

So, what is the way forward? As already stated, I have been crying at the top of my voice for a good while. I feel drained and worn-out. Despite all my effort, no one appears even a wee bit concerned.

I am now having second thoughts. I think at the end of the day, it is my own welfare that has to be paramount. Yes, I have to consider my own well-being above everything else. If I keep on crying and crying, I may lose all my strength and eventually drop dead! There have been times in the past when I wished I could return from where I came from.

The uncertainty as to what will await me on my return has in the meantime led to a change of heart. I heard Father telling one of his friends the other day that "the devil you know is better than an angel you don't know!" Well, I better draw wisdom from the quote and face the future—with or without breastmilk! So, I have calmed down now. Instead of leaving me alone, Kwaku has returned.

"So you have stopped yelling? I thought you were going to continue crying till the end of time?"

I have decided not to respond to this needless provocation! I thought Kwaku would allow the matter to rest. But no, he has chosen to repeat the same words. I think I better walk away rather than allow myself to be infuriated any further. So, I am walking away from the scene! I have now taken my position under the shadow of a big mango tree growing in our compound—I am enjoying a peaceful spell from the near-permanent commotions of our home.

Concerning, Kwaku; I have so far considered him to be nicer than Kwame. Well, based on the behaviour just displayed towards me, I am no longer certain about the matter.

*

Hey, someone, please help! This is ridiculous! Just as I was walking around our compound with a piece of bread just given me by Mother, one of our goats emerged from nowhere and snatched it from my hands!

This is not the first time I have experienced such rudeness! Since I started eating solid food, our animals have not ceased to annoy me. They seem to have earmarked me up as the weakest link, the vulnerable one who cannot resist them.

The other day it was the cockerel that made away with a chunk of food in my bowl. Now it is the turn of the insolent goats! They are particularly rude to me! They have been disrespectful to me in instances far too many to list here! I am fed up with them! No way am I going to tolerate any further brazen disregard for civility and manners—not from *any* of the animals! So, I have decided to give the offender a chase to remember! I will surely give him lessons in good behaviour should I lay hands on him!

So, I am running as fast as my legs can carry me! "Hey Kwame and Kwaku, please help me catch this insolent fellow, who keeps disturbing my peace!" I am getting no response. Everyone here seems to be occupied with their own business. Not even the cries of the most vulnerable person bother them! I find it very strange indeed. "Hey Kwame, please join in the chase!"

Ach, Kwame, he pretends not to hear me! Well, I will have to learn to fight my own battle. It appears the motto in this household is—each one for himself and God for us all!

Aargh! Poor me, I have tripped and fallen—on the hard ground! It's really painful! I have decided to give up the chase. "You impudent animal! Your day will come! I will surely catch you the next time round!"

I ask myself—why for God's sake are these nasty animals left to roam our compounds with impunity? If only we had just our own naughty animals to contend with! But no, they come from all parts of the settlement. Indeed, from observing the settlement from my perch on Mother's back as she takes me round, it is clear that none of the homes in the village is demarcated from one another by way of a wall or fence or what have you. And since almost every household keeps animals, they move around the village without any hindrance.

2L

SIBLING MEALTIME RIVALRY

We are having a meal. As I mentioned earlier on, all the three boys at home eat from the same plate. There are some birds flying above us. They look just like the bird that made a nose dive the other day and stole one of our chickens. Everyone at home was really furious on that occasion.

"Hey everyone, take a look at those birds!" I cry out at the top of my voice. "They may well be planning another attack on our chicks!"

"Stop shouting!" Kwaku shouts back at me in a loud voice. I won't take it without comment; after all, I was doing what I consider proper, sounding a note of warning for everyone.

"Don't shout at me!" I counter.

"I am not shouting at you. I am just teaching you some good manners."

"What do you mean by that?"

"It is expected of us not to talk whilst eating!"

"Who told you that?"

"Well, you just ask Mama, if I am lying!"

"Mama, Kwaku is telling me not to talk whilst eating; is he right?"

"Yes indeed; children are not supposed to talk whilst eating!"

"Why not?"

"If you do, the spirits will come and take away your food, so you will never get satisfied!"

"Spirits? Where will they come from?"

"Keep eating and don't ask too many questions!"

"I just don't understand why everyone keeps on telling me this and that without giving any proper explanation!"

"Why don't you just shut up and don't let your saliva pour into the soup. No one wants to eat that!"

"But I saw your saliva drop in the soup just as you shouted!"

"Hey boys, will you just stop arguing and enjoy your food in peace!"

Well, I respect Mother, so I will keep my mouth shut and not prolong matters any further!

*

"That is not fair!"

"What is not fair?"

"You have taken the best portion of the fish and handed me only the head!"

"But you are the most junior—accept what you get!"

"No, that is not fair; I will report you to Mother!"

"Go ahead and report!"

"Mama, look! They have given me only the head of the fish! Useless for eating!"

"Kwame, be fair and don't cheat him."

"I have not cheated him, just have a look. I can give him only what I have. It is your fault. You have, as usual, given the best portion to Father. Now what do you expect of me!"

"Hey, don't be rude to me, boy!"

"I am not being rude. I am just repeating what we have been complaining about all along! Instead of listening to us, you keep telling us: 'It is our custom to reserve the best portion of the meat for fathers!' Now everyone is blaming me for cheating on the meat, when in reality there is not enough to go round!"

*

This argument concerning the fair distribution of meat during meals—it comes up almost on a daily basis. A solution, in my view, would be for each one of us to eat from a separate bowl. But everyone is saying: "Brothers must eat from the same bowl." Is that the real motive, or is it because we don't have enough bowls at home to go round? Whatever the reason, being the youngest of the *team*, I have no option but to rely on the sense of fairness of my older *team mates.*

2M

THE TRIUMPHANT ARRIVAL OF PRINCESS LATE!

Something worthy of reporting happened today! Indeed, it reminds me of the day of my arrival in my new home. As I mentioned earlier on, Mother's belly has of late become bigger and bigger. I need not repeat what I mentioned earlier about me being forced to stop breast-feeding! Though Mother did not expressly mention to my face that the decision to stop breastfeeding me had anything to do with the expected newcomer, it was clear to me that in fact was the case.

As if in preparation for the expected event, one of Mother's cousins arrived from Amantia. Kwaku told me, just as in my case, the same individual arrived just a few days ahead of my birth. When I woke up in the morning I looked out for Mother, but she was nowhere to be found. I became panicky and began to cry.

"What is the matter with you, cry-baby?" Kwame inquired.

"Mamaa, Mamaa? Where is Mother!" I kept on crying.

"In the bathroom!"

On hearing that, I made my way towards our makeshift family bath-room, a rectangular structure fenced with bamboo, and exposed at the top to the free tropical sky.

"Get back!" Kwaku shouted at me!

"Why?"

"Children are not allowed there!"

"Why not?" I insisted.

"Aunt Akosua Worae will not permit you to proceed any further!" and Kwaku whisked me from the ground.

I protested vehemently—to no avail.

After crying for a while, I am now quiet. I am sitting quietly on the lap of the relative I just referred to.

From the conversation going on around me, I got to know that a new baby was on the way. Maame Gyamfuah and Maame Adwoa Adeye, two elderly women from our neighbourhood, were said to be with her, assisting her in delivering my new brother—or perhaps sister.

A good while has elapsed since Aunt got hold of me. She in the meantime offered me something to eat—the usual *ampesi*—which I have thankfully accepted.

Hey, one of the ladies attending to Mother has rushed out of the little enclosure! She appears quite apprehensive. She runs to Kwaku who happens to be standing not far from us: "Little boy, run as quickly as you can to the home of Papa Osei. Ask him to please proceed here as quickly as he can—we need his assistance urgently!"

Just as she turns to go back to the bathroom, Aunty draws near to her and asks: "Anything to worry about?"

"Quite challenging. Let's keep on praying!" she replies and walks quickly away.

Not long after Kwaku leaves, Papa Osei comes rushing to our home. Soon he joins the others in the little enclosure already referred to. About half an hour after the arrival of the 'village doctor' I can hear the screams of a baby! It is followed almost immediately by the claps and shouts of joy of the three adults attending to Mother.

Several minutes later, Mother, who seems to be in terrible pain, emerges from the bathroom turned labour ward, assisted by the two women. Tenderly, they lead her into the bedroom. She remains there with our newly arrived sister for the rest of the day.

*

The privilege I have enjoyed since my arrival in my new environment is over. Indeed, I was expecting it. I thought however that the loss of attention afforded me would be gradual and not as immediate and radical as it has turned out to be.

It all boils down to the fact that the new arrival to our homestead is girl.

I still remember the first comments Father made when he introduced himself to me the very first time –"We were expecting a girl. Never mind though, you are here with us so welcome home!" Now everyone at home is overjoyed!

Does it have anything to do with Mother's extreme joy at the arrival of our sister? That may well account for the sudden burst of energy, joy and exuberance in Mother. I recall vividly that at the time of my arrival it took Mother several days to regain her strength; not this time though! It is barely a day since she delivered our sister and yet she is going about her usual activities as if nothing at all has happened!

*

Mother rarely takes her eyes off the new arrival to our home. Indeed, she hardly gives her away to anyone, not even the relative who visited purposely to help her. Furthermore, she keeps on offering her breast milk all the time, even when the little sister seems uninterested.

Am I being jealous, perhaps? I don't know for sure. What is certain is that I am not amused that all of a sudden all attention has shifted away from me towards my sister.

Like everyone else, I have had the chance to take a look at my sister. She appears very fair-coloured, just like Mother. Kwame tells me her pale skin colour will in time change to assume a darker hue, just as in our case—let's wait and see.

Father has just arrived from work on the field, and he is also over-joyed—yes, euphoric! He tenderly picked up the little baby: "Oh, what a sweet looking girl!" he began. "I am speechless to describe her beauty!"

The little one appears unimpressed and is crying loudly.

"Keep quiet my sweet little princess."

"Papa, what about calling her Princess Late—the beautiful princess who delayed her coming to the very last minute?!" Kwaku has suggested.

"A brilliant idea!" Father concurs. "So, everyone please join me in welcoming Princess Late into our midst!"

*

Mother has yearned for a girl, not only to keep her company, but also to help in the household chores. I have my reservations, though. The way she is being adored and showered with praises from all sides, she may well become self-conceited, nurturing a feeling of being above reproach and so become lazybones.

*

I can hear the screams of my little sister from the room she shares with Mother; this is beyond the ordinary! What is happening to our little princess just a day after her arrival in our midst? I am inquisitive—I will go and have a look. I have now arrived at the scene.

My goodness, what have they done to the poor little one! They have indeed inflicted several cut wounds to both cheeks of her face! Why didn't they leave it with a single cut to the right side of the face as in my case?

Ouch! It looks really scary! My little sister must be in excruciating pain!

Mother as usual is trying to appease her with breastmilk—to no avail! She appears inconsolable. That does not surprise me, judging from what has been done to her. I will find out from Mother why she allowed her to undergo such torture.

"Why have you done that to her?"

"We have to do it to prevent her from going back to where she came from!"

"Going back to where she came from?"

"Yes!"

"I don't understand!"

"I don't expect you to understand, even if I were to explain it in simple terms. It is indeed too complex for a child to understand."

"Just tell me—maybe I will understand!"

"Well, I will try to explain in words that hopefully will make sense to you. We have over the years yearned for a girl. Two girls who came before you passed away shortly after their birth. Inflicting several cuts in the face is our only means of stopping her passing away, indeed from returning to where she came from."

"Really?"

"Yes indeed. It is the general belief that inflicting several tribal marks on her face will prevent her from returning to where she came from!"

"But why?"

"Because she will appear so facially disfigured the person watching the gate to the realm she came from will not permit her entry, so she will be forced to stay with us!"

"Do you believe that?"

"Well, that is the general belief here. I cannot believe otherwise."

"Hmm!"

"What do you mean by Hmm!"

"Difficult to believe."

"I don't expect someone of your age to believe it. Indeed, I wouldn't have explained it to you if you hadn't asked about it.

"Just to make my explanation complete—Apart from the marks, she will also be called Donkor. Donkor means a servant. Since she has been declared a servant, no-one will want to accept her back where she came from. The several marks on her face together with the name have the effect of forcing her to remain with us for a very long time—at least that is the general belief here."

The ordeal is now over for my little sister. The stranger who inflicted the marks has left our compound. My little sister has, despite the cuts, fallen asleep.

*

Ach, today has reminded me of an incident that happened a few months ago. It involved my brother Kwame. As mother was in the process of breastfeeding me, he came and stood beside her.

"I also want to enjoy some breastmilk!" he declared.

"Your time has passed, my friend. You had the opportunity to enjoy breastmilk for almost two years! Now it's the turn of your little brother!"

Not happy with the answer, he tried forcefully to pull my mouth away from the nipple. I protested with a scream! That led Mother to lose her temper; in the process she pushed him slightly. Kwame unexpectedly lost his balance and fell to the ground, sustaining quite a deep cut to the forehead. As the blood oozed from the wound Mother put me aside to attend to him. Feeling deserted, I began crying at the top of my voice. Poor mother, she had to find a way of dealing with two troublesome children at the same time. She called Kwaku to come to her assistance. As he stood "guard" around me, Mother cleaned the wound and treated it with the paste Kawku hurriedly prepared from the leaves of a plant growing along the perimeters of our home.

*

I now find myself in a situation similar to that of Kwame. Ever since the arrival of my sister, I have noted, not without consternation, that all attention has been shifted to her. Was it due to a feeling of neglect? I cannot say for sure. What is beyond dispute is that as she was in the process of being breastfed, I approached Mother and without warning pulled my sister's lips away from the nipple!

As might be expected, the matter did not go well with my little sister, who began to cry at the top of her voice. Just as in the case already narrated, Mother instinctively pushed me away. Unlike the case of Kwame, however, I did not fall down. Notwithstanding that, I felt deeply saddened and as well as neglected for most of the day.

2N

TOY CARS MADE IN AN AFRICAN VILLAGE

If everything goes well, I will acquire my own toy car next week—not one manufactured in a factory, I must stress. No, my parents have made it clear to me they are not in a position to purchase factory-made toys for us.

As a matter of fact, I would not have come by the idea of requesting them to purchase a factory-made toy car for me, but for the fact that one of my cousins living in Akim Oda, our district capital, arrived in the village on a visit. On seeing his wonderful plastic toy car, I approached Mama and Papa to request one. They made it clear that they had never purchased toy cars for any of their children and that they were not prepared to set a precedent in my case even if they had the means to do so.

So far I have been allowed occasionally, by both Kwame and Kwaku, to play with their respective toy cars.

I hear you ask: "You just mentioned that your parents are not in a position to purchase toy cars for their children; so how did Kwame and Kwaku come by their cars?"

The answer is that we have a cousin called Kwaku Driver. I suppose he got his alias "Driver" by virtue of his obsession with toy cars. He does not purchase them from shops—no, he builds them with raw material growing in the woods surrounding our little community! For the body of the vehicle, he makes use of the fibre from the branches of the raffia palm. He makes the wheels from the roots of the Onyina tree. That is all that I have been told by my brothers. I cannot produce any details as to how he goes about building his cars making use of those raw materials.

He is so kind-hearted he readily builds them for the boys in the community—for free. The only pre-condition is that they or their parents have to provide him with the required raw materials.

After Kwaku had joined other boys to fetch the raw materials, our cousin produced two toy Bedford trucks and presented one to each of them.

A few days ago I was walking beside Mother on the street when we came across my cousin on the street. Mother addressed Kwaku Driver:

"Kwaku, when will it be the turn for my little one to get his toy car?"

"Oh, I nearly forgot about him. I am actually free now. If someone would fetch the raw material, I will be happy to build one for him."

On hearing this I cried at the top of my voice:

"Mama, I will go and fetch the material myself!"

"That is not possible my dear. You are barely three years old—too young to take on the assignment."

Next, she turned to Kwaku Driver:

"Thanks for your offer. I will try and talk one of his elder brothers into fetching them on his behalf."

After much persuasion, Mother has managed to prevail on Kwaku to collect the raw materials on my behalf.

*

Kwaku is just back from the woods. He was not out alone. He joined a group of his peers who were on a mission to harvest material for their toy vehicles. As I am making this entry, Kwaku Driver is now busy at work building my toy lorry! At my request, he is building a Bedford truck!

*

20

SCHOOL OF PERSONAL HYGIENE

Has it got to do with the arrival of my sister? Whatever the reason, I am being asked to do almost everything myself. For example, whereas previously Mother has been washing and creaming me, I have now been asked to do so on my own. Kwame has been asked to mentor me till I become self-sufficient in my new role.

I have already mentioned the make-shift bathroom where I first emerged into this world. It is usually used by adults. Children like Kwaku and Kwame usually wash outside, in the open air.

One might think each one of us at home possesses our individual toiletry bags—not at all! The common practise is for the males to share the same toiletries whilst the females do the same. So, there is a common bathing sponge for the boys. We also share the same drying towel.

The same thing applies to the female members of the family. Up to the arrival of Princess Late, Mother had everything for herself—but no longer. So, Kwame and I are standing in front of an aluminium bucket filled with lukewarm water. Kwame has finished washing; being the elder he has the first right of use of our common washing sponge.

He is pouring almost the whole content of the bucket over himself. That has caught the attention of Mother who is sitting on a chair a few metres away breastfeeding Princess Late.

"Hey Kwame, don't use all the water! You've got to leave some for your little brother."

"There is still quite a lot left."

"Not really, my friend." I am challenging him!

My eyes have met those of a group of teenage girls from the neigh-bourhood who are walking just along the perimeters of our compound on their way to fetch water from the community well, which happens to be located a stone's throw from our home.

"Keep your eyes away!" Kwame cries aloud to them.

"How did you know we were watching you!" one of them shouts back.

Frankly, I am not happy with the idea of exposing my everything to the whole world! I made that known to Papa and Ma the other day, to which I was told I will be permitted to use the bathroom when I am past ten years old. Well, I have no choice but to live with the situation for now.

"Hey boy, don't you know how to wash yourself? Do you have to spend the whole time washing only your big belly? You also have to wash your back, and your '*down below*'!" That is Kwame. He is actually neglecting his duty! He was asked to guide me! Instead of taking hold of the sponge and demonstrating to me the best way to go about the matter, he is just standing idle by and engaging in a running commentary!

"Hey Kwame, help your little brother wash his back! How do you expect him to do so alone?" Mother! She has a good command of every-thing that happens under her watch—always!

"I am happy to help him wash his back—not his down below though! It is not my job to wash his backside!" That is Kwame being cheeky!

*

Well, I have managed it—my first wash done without Mother's help. That just leaves creaming—but I just don't like the scent of this yellow-looking cream! Kwaku told me it's called shea-butter. He went on to state that the cream is produced in the north of the country from the fruits of the shea butter tree. Not believing him, I asked Father for confirmation.

"That is exactly the case," Father told me.

Everyone in the village seems to be using it. I just don't know how and where it is made. Why don't the producers mix it with a wee bit of perfume at the time of production. As it is now, the scent isn't lovely at all. Well, I don't have any choice but to cream myself with whatever balm is available.

Why have I developed such an affection for my tummy? I just wonder! The fact remains that just as I devoted too much time to washing my belly, I have also subconsciously devoted a good deal of time creaming my abdomen. My curious behaviour has not gone unnoticed!

"Mama, just take a look at your little boy! He is applying the whole container full of cream to his big belly!"

"Hey Kofi," Mother calls out to me, "haven't you been paying attention to how I have been creaming you?"

I have chosen not to reply. Mother has now turned to my senior brother: "Kwame, please help your junior brother cream himself, in particular his back." This time Kwame does as instructed without comment.

Now I am finished with creaming, I need to put on my clothes.

"Mama, any clean slips for me?"

"What do you mean by clean?"

"Something that has been washed clean; the one I have been wearing is dirty.

"Be satisfied with what you have! You think I am a machine? I don't have the time and energy to wash your dirty linen on a daily basis, okay? You can choose to do so when you grow up!"

Well, there is no option left for me. I have only one slip and it is dirty; yet I have to wear it until Mother finds the time to wash it. I am not blaming her though; she is doing her best under very challenging circumstances. So, I have my slip on now. I have nothing for the top. I would surely benefit from a T-shirt or an easy-to-wear short-sleeved shirt—but there's none of those! What I have is a piece of wax-print cloth that I wrap around my body. The easiest way to walk around with it is to tie both ends around the neck.

The weather here is so warm, hardly any of the boys I see on the street ever wear any tops. The same thing applies to the young girls. For reasons that I don't understand, the bigger girls always go about with their tops covered.

*

Another first in my life! I am, just like my other brothers, going to start brushing my teeth. My big brothers are able to produce their own charcoal brushes; Mother has helped me produce my own. I just want to explain to the understanding of those not familiar with the process, how the charcoal brush is *manufactured*. The first component is the stalk by which the finger of a green plantain is attached to the whole bundle. This is cut or slit from the rest of the finger. It is then beaten into a brush, usually with the help of a stone crucible. The second component is a piece of charcoal. This is beaten into a powder. A few drops of water are added to the powder to turn it into a semi-solid paste, just as in the case of a factory-made toothpaste.

The charcoal paste is spread on the brush already described. The cleaning of the teeth with the toothbrush and toothpaste made in our home can now begin! Yesterday Mother demonstrated to me how to brush my teeth with the charcoal paste; today I am giving it a try.

Ach, just as I am about to start, a couple of goats have gathered around me! "Hey good friends, this is no food for you—but you may still watch me as I brush my teeth with charcoal for the first-time!"

They seem to have understood, for they are not moving an inch! The session lasted a couple of minutes. That should be enough. I need some water to rinse my mouth.

That has been accomplished. I will go to the sleeping room to find a mirror and have a look. Ha, the goats have left, but two little sheep are still following me. "Hey good friends, it's all over, you can disperse!"

No, they wouldn't leave! These sheep and goats, they are really becoming my friends. The sheep are easy to control, not so the goats though. I should be tactful in dealing with them though, or they may think I want to discriminate against them.

I am now looking into the mirror. "Surprise, surprise! How indeed did the dark charcoal brush manage to turn my teeth into such sparkling white!"

This is a really ingenious method of keeping the teeth sparkling white! The only downside is that I will have to prepare the brush and the paste on a daily basis, since there is no way of storing it beyond a few hours. I will find out from the big ones in the family why that is not the case.

Kwame is here, so I will start with him.

"Kwame, come on, why are we not able to store the charcoal brush for future use?"

"I have no idea; you better ask Mother."

"Okay, I will find out from her."

"Hey Mama, why are we not able to keep the charcoal brush for later use?"

"You ask your father; he will be here very soon."

"Why does everyone seem to be pushing the question to another?"

"What else do you expect me to do? I'd rather refer you to someone who might have an idea than to tell you an untruth."

"Alternatively, you can come up with your own solution to the problem!"

"You mark it on the wall. I will surely come up with a solution when I grow up."

"That is once again the Mr Big Mouth speaking!" Kwaku retorted.

"Why Mr Big Mouth?"

"Because of your big talk!"

"This is no big talk."

"Well, let's watch and see."

"Exactly!" Kwaku remarked.

*

Kwabena is back home from school. Whereas I have been given the charcoal brush to clean my teeth, Kwabena is doing so with a piece of wood! It appears he has first to chew on the end of a small piece of wood. Holding on firmly to the other end, he brushes his teeth making use of the tuft created by the earlier chewing.

I don't understand why I have to brush my teeth with a charcoal brush whilst Kwabena is using a chewing stick, so I'm confronting him for an explanation.

"The answer is simple, my friend; your teeth are not strong enough to chew on the hard stick. It may well break into pieces if you attempt to do so! You just exercise patience, my dear little brother. It won't be very long before you'll be able to brush your teeth just like us!"

If Kwame or Kwaku had explained the matter to me, I wouldn't have believed him. Not so Kwabena. Everyone seems to hold him in high regard!

*

I'm trying to play the big brother to my sister.

"Mama, please give me Adwoa. I want to carry her on my back."

"No, that is something for girls and mothers."

"Why?"

"Because they are the ones who bear children in later life."

"Bear children in later life? How does that happen?"

"Oh, away with your many questions! If you want something to do, just pick up the hoe and clear the weed on the compound! That's a boy's duty!"

2P

AN EVER-RECURRING MENACE FOR UNPROTECTED FEET

Oh my goodness, this problem, yes, this tormentor has returned! What tormentor, you might ask? How do I explain it to everyone's understanding? Well, in the Twi language we call it *apropro*. Kwabena, our resident academic, said the condition is known as athlete's foot in English. Whether that is true or not, I don't know. But the fact is, it's a recurring condition that afflicts everyone at home on a regular basis. The worst season however is during the rainy season. That has led us to suspect it has something to do with muddy terrain. I am becoming tired of pointing out that my brothers and I have to go about barefoot. Even as regards Mama and Papa—even though they usually go about wearing crude homemade sandals, their feet are still subject to exposure to mud.

Though the compound of our home is covered for the most part with gravel, some portions tend to become muddy when it rains. The most exposure to mud however occurs when we visit our farmlands.

Apropro usually affects the forefoot area, especially the spaces between the toes. No one at home has any idea what exactly causes it. Since, as already mentioned, it is associated with mud, I usually ask myself—is it caused by something hidden in the sludge? It usually begins with itchiness to the skin. The itching forces me to scratch the affected area. The more I scratch, the more it itches! At times I spend a good while scratching, scratching and scratching. In due time the affected area begins to sting and burn as well!

In such moments, I ask Mother if there is no remedy to help break the vicious cycle. "Remedy! You must be a dreamer! I have since childhood suffered from this recurring menace. No one has told me about any cure!"

On this occasion, the *apropro* affliction has turned really bad. It is not affecting myself alone—indeed almost every member of the family is afflicted. A stranger who visits our home may well think there is a scratching competition going on between us!

How I wish I could be permitted to stay away from the farm to help with the healing. But then, how can I claim this privilege for myself when everyone is affected.

So, poor me, I cannot help but accompany my parents to the farm despite the awful state of my feet.

2Q

THE LITTLE BABY WHO DID NOT MAKE IT

Everyone appears sad at home; it is indeed really upsetting. I am lost for words. What happened, you ask?

Three days ago a stranger arrived at our house. She was carrying a small brown traveller's bag in her right hand. A little baby was fastened to her back. Mother welcomed her wholeheartedly to our home. From what I later gleaned from Mother's conversation with the stranger, she hailed from Amantia, which readers might recall is Mother's village of birth.

I did not understand every detail of their conversation. What I understood was that she was in our village to seek help for her sick baby boy. Her baby indeed needed help. Yes, even though I am not big enough to understand everything around me, I realized something was seriously wrong with him. He appeared more like a sack of bones to me—yes, one could just about count all his bones! Was it because he was so emaciated? It might well be the case, for his head appeared too big for his little body to carry. His eyes could hardly be seen, for both appeared sunken into his head.

He appeared so unwell, he seemed even to have lost the energy to cry. The little sound that came from him reminded me of the *meow, meow* sounds of our little cat rather than that of a baby. After resting a while, Mother fastened my little sister to her back and headed for the centre of the village accompanied by our visitor. I refused to stay behind at home and joined them. On Mother's advice she carried the little one in her arms instead of on her back, for Mother felt it was unsafe to fasten him to the back since he appeared so frail.

Where were we heading for? After walking a short distance along the main street of our little settlement, Mother left the main road and headed for a building which appeared familiar to me. It happened to be the home of Papa Osei, who is regarded as a kind of doctor in the village.

He welcomed us wholeheartedly to his home. After exchanging cordial greetings, he offered us a seat. Shortly after taking her seat Mother began:

"This is my cousin, Adwoa Nyame. She arrived a short while ago from Amantia to seek your help for her sick baby. It is our hope you will be able to help the little one."

"Of course, I will do my best," Papa Osei began after a short silence. "You must realize however that there is a limit to what I can do, especially in this case." At that stage, he turned to the mother and asked: "Mama, why did you wait so long?"

"Sir, we were trying to raise the money."

"I don't personally put much emphasis on money. What is important for me is the health of my patients. Even now, if you are unable to pay upfront, I will be happy with instalment payments."

"Thank you so much. You are a real angel!"

"Thanks for your compliment."

Next, he took the little one in his arms, looked sternly in his eyes, and began reciting something which sounded like Latin to my ears. He then returned the little one to his mother.

"Please wait for a while as I go to the adjoining woods to collect the ingredients needed for the herbal concoction," he announced.

True to his words, he returned after a short while, a small jute carrier bag hanging from his shoulder. He poured the contents into a plastic bowl. He then handed the container to Mother with the following instructions:

"This mixture of leaves, seeds, barks of various trees are the ingredients required to prepare the herbal medicine which hopefully will lead to his recovery. You have to pour the contents into a black clay pot.

Please note—it should be a black clay pot and nothing else. Fill the pot to about three quarters with water and boil the contents for about fifteen minutes. Allow the boiled mixture to cool down before dispensing. You are to dispense a small teaspoonful three times a day, morning, afternoon and evening—just before meals."

Mother thought he was done with us and begged permission to leave.

"No, I am not done yet! Please wait a moment as I fetch yet another therapy component." Saying that he made for his room, returning a few minutes later with a small plastic container bearing a metal lid. He turned the lid open to show Mother the contents—a yellowish-coloured cream.

"Apply the cream, thinly, mornings and evenings to the whole body," he instructed.

Mother and our visitor both thanked him most sincerely for his kindness. A short while later we were back on the street, heading back home. On reaching home, Mother helped our visitor prepare and dispense the herbal medication as instructed. The baby was so weak that even swallowing the liquid seemed an uphill struggle.

*

Mother offered the boys' room to our visitor. Kwame and Kwaku came to sleep in our room—on a mat spread on the bare floor in front of the wooden bed. On waking up the next day, I realized the cries of the little one had become even more faint; he could hardly move.

On noticing the marked deterioration in the condition of the little one, Mother grasped the baby into her arms and urged her cousin to come along with her.

"Where are you going in such a hurry?" Kwame inquired.

"We are taking him back to Papa Osei for further attention!"

Was I being too selfish, thinking only about my well-being rather than that of the little one? I will leave others to make their own judgement in the matter. In any case, I became concerned Mother was deserting me for good and I began screaming at the top of my voice.

Mother was unimpressed. She appeared much too concerned for the well-being of the critically unwell baby to be bothered by the antics of selfish cry-baby.

"Kwaku, take good care of him! We need to bring the little one to the attention of Papa Osei without delay."

After screaming for a while, I was overtaken by sleep. I cannot say for how long I slept. Kwaku managed to carry me to the sleeping room after I had fallen asleep, for I woke up on my bed. As usual I began crying on waking up. Kwaku came to pick me up. Seeing no sign of Mother, I kept on screaming.

"Hey, you better keep quiet or I'll show you the red!"

Fortunately, shortly after being thus threatened, to my relief Mother and our visitor returned.

"Why did you keep away so long?" were the first words that issued from Kwame's mouth.

Even before Mama could utter a word, Kwaku turned to her and asked:

"Where is the baby?"

Initially Mother remained silent.

"Mama, where have you left the little one?" Kwaku persisted.

"He did not make it," Mother replied, barely able to control her tears.

"What do you mean by that?"

"He has gone where he came from!"

"Gone where he came from? What do you mean by that?"

"Ach my dear little one; you are too young to understand such matters!"

"The same place where Grandma has left for?"

"Yes indeed."

"But I heard it is only the very elderly who return to such places after a long stay on earth?"

"No, that is not the case. Anyone who comes to the world, regardless of their age, can do so at any time."

"Will it be my turn next?" Kwame inquired.

"I don't know! It is not up to humans to decide."

"But who decides?"

"The One up there."

"Up where?"

"In the skies!" Mother pointed to the heavens.

"I cannot see anyone."

"He cannot be seen with our naked eyes."

"Why not?"

"You are too young to understand everything my dear. You best leave the matter for now. I need to attend to our visitor!"

After spending the night with us, our visitor, who remained inconsolable for the rest of the day, left us and returned to where she came from, leaving the mortal remains of her little one to rest in our little cemetery, as I was told.

YEAR 3

3A

"SMUGGLED INJECTION" WREAKING HAVOC AT HOME

I have to write this down—to be sure, I really have to write this down. This is a really awful experience, a really awful experience I must record.

I have been unwell for a while. I felt my body warming up and my head aching. In the end my body became so hot it felt like I was on fire. Based on my previous experience, I thought I would undergo the usual therapy rituals—being given herbal medicine to drink followed perhaps by enema, a ginger suppository, a bath with herbal concomitants, etc.

Ach! the burning ginger suppository! The thought of it sends goose pimples all over my body. Strangely, scary as it is, I have somehow gotten used to it. But that will not be the case now. In the course of the morning Mother called Kwaku and began:

"Run to the house of Kwadwo Amoh and tell him one of the children is unwell, and I need his help."

Kwaku did as instructed. He returned a short while later, a well-built man in his mid-thirties walking alongside him.

Mother politely offered the newcomer a seat. After conversing with him for a short while, she directed him to the boys' sleeping room.

Father arrived a short while later, one of his junior brothers walking beside him. Shortly after Father's arrival, Mother took my hands and led me to the room where the stranger was, Father and Uncle following us. I began to wonder what the matter was that had drawn my parents and the two other adults together. I wouldn't have to wait long for an answer!

No sooner had Father and Uncle stepped into the room than Mother pulled down my slip to expose my buttocks.

"What is the matter?" I inquired.

"Uncle will give you medicine to cure you," Mother replied, pointing to the stranger.

At that juncture, Mother, Father and Uncle took hold of me! Mother grasped both my hands, then Father took care of my trunk whilst Uncle held my buttocks firmly. Then it happened! The stranger took from his bag a syringe with a sharp pointed needle and without delay injected a yellow-looking fluid into my right buttocks!

Have I experienced anything so painful in my life? Definitely not! There were two aspects to the pain. First, there was the aching I felt from the needle piercing my body that lasted only a short while. Then there was the burning sensation which I guess was caused by the medicine being injected. It persisted for a good while thereafter. I don't know exactly for how long I screamed! It did indeed continue for a considerable while.

The stress from the pain, the effect of the medicine on my body, and the loud screams appeared too much for my body—mercifully soon I was overcome by sleep.

When I awoke from sleep I was lying in bed in our room. I was not alone though; a couple of our goats were present and were busily feeding on the stock of plantain fingers being kept in the room. Just then Kwaku, who had been dispatched by Mother to check on me, entered the room. Frightened by the sudden arrival of the unexpected intruder, the audacious four-legged beasts bolted out of the room.

*

The pain from the site of the injection persisted for three days nonstop! I am only hoping and praying it does not develop into a boil. Furthermore, it is my hope this will be my last-ever encounter with the individual who inflicted me with such awful pain.

It's odd, quite unusual, I should say. Everyone at home has been referring to the individual who gave me the injection as "doctor". They seem to be putting him on a par with the friendly medical team who took care of me when I was a little baby. How can this resident of our village, yes someone I saw working on his farm the other day as we returned from work on our field, be a doctor? I just wonder.

*

I am very concerned for Mother. She is our rock. Now she can hardly move. The problem is with her right leg. She can hardly walk on it.

It all began a few days ago. She was not feeling well, so the doctor I wrote about, I mean the one who inserted that terrible needle into my buttocks, came around and did to Mother exactly what he did to me! I must say that was not the first time he has treated her—no, he has been here a couple of times in the recent past. This time, I think things have gone terribly wrong. She can hardly bear weight on the leg where the injection was administered. Kwame is saying that the place is swollen; personally, I am too scared to have a look.

Some are saying she should travel to the hospital. This time I think there is no issue with money. Father has recently sold a few bags of cocoa beans, so he should have sufficient money to pay for her treatment. But the real problem is how to transport her to hospital. She is in such pain that the general consensus is that it is not advisable to transport her on one of the usually congested vehicles, not to mention the fact that much of the road leading to the hospital is ridden with potholes. So, we are resorting to traditional medicine for her cure.

*

Thank goodness, the boil that formed over the injection spot on Mother's buttock has burst open! It discharged a good amount of dark red blood. I was scared at the sight of the blood. Not so Kwaku, who drew closer to have a good look without showing any sign of panic!

*

Father has sent Kwaku on an errand to purchase medicine for Mama—not to the home of the so-called doctor who caused the problem in the first place. No, he has been dispatched to the home of another resident of the community. I have heard that the two medicines involved are known respectively as M&B and APC.

Kwaku is back. He has two small packs in his hands. He has handed both to Papa. Papa has unwrapped them. Each contains several white tablets. He has picked two tablets from one pack and has presented them to Mother to swallow, making use of a cup of water in his hands—which she has gratefully accepted.

Papa has now selected a few tablets from the second pack. He has placed them in a small crucible and is grinding them. After grinding them for a while, the tablets have turned into powder. I thought he was going to dissolve the powder in water and present the solution to her to drink. But no, he has a different plan. He has instead mixed the powder with shea butter cream. Hey, what is he up to? Applying the cream mixed with the medicine directly to the wound? How does he know it can lead to a cure? Well, Father might as well refer to himself as a doctor!

*

It has been exactly a week since Mother's boil burst. She is back to her former self. She is able to walk freely, though she appears to be in some discomfort.

What is she up to? She has already put-on clothes she usually wears when heading for the field. I thought she would stay away from the farm for a while to allow the wound sufficient time to heal completely! That doesn't seem to be the case. "Mama, don't tell me you are getting ready to visit the farm already! You need rest!"

I thought it was me alone that harboured such reservations! But no; Kwaku is thinking likewise.

"Thanks for your concern, my dear," Mother responded with a smile. "Don't worry, I am okay."

"No, you are not!"

"Be at ease, boy. I will quickly visit the farmland that's closest to home, harvest some plantains, cassava and vegetables and come straight back home. I wouldn't take the trouble upon myself if I didn't have to. As it is, we have almost nothing to sustain us."

I am not that old. I have however known Mother long enough to be aware that hardly anyone can change her mind once she sets out to get something done.

3B

A HEAD- BALANCING ACT

Today I had an opportunity to realise what I have all along been yearning for, namely to carry things on my own head.

I have indeed been fascinated by the ability of others, including children who are only a bit bigger than me, to manage to carry items on their heads. Some managed to balance the loads on their heads and walk considerable distances without supporting them—not even with one hand! For the last several days I have been impatient with my parents, as I have kept on pressurizing them to allow me to give it a try!

"You are too young to do so," has been their reply so far.

On not a few occasions, such denials were met with loud screams of protest on my part. Well, today, at last, Mama has caved in to my incessant demands.

"Okay, you can have a try. This particular farm is very near home, so you won't have far to walk." A short silence followed before Mother continued: "As a start, I will give you a finger of plantain to carry home."

"What? Only one finger of plantain?"

"Yes of course, what else did you expect?"

"That is nothing for me! Give us a bunch; yes, a whole bunch!"

"A whole bunch? My goodness—even your big brother Kwaku is not able to carry that much! So, for now you start with a single finger. In time you can try a few fingers, then a hand and finally the whole bunch."

"Okay, okay, you can give me a finger for now!"

So now I am bearing a finger of plantain on my head! I am walking ahead of Mother. Kwame and Kwaku are far ahead of us. Kwaku has turned to Mother:

211

"Hey Mother, take care of your little one; we are forging ahead! We cannot tolerate this guy who is walking as slow as a tortoise."

My big brothers! They are behaving as if they were never at my stage of development! Instead of cheering and motivating me, encouraging me, they are taunting and upsetting me!

3C

GINGER SUPPOSITORIES AND A DARE-DEVIL CHILD

Ach, I lost my composure today! I am not very happy to admit it, but, well, it did happen.

The whole issue revolved around the size of my head and belly. My peers have all the time been taunting me concerning the matter. They are saying I possess a disproportionately big head and stomach!

What on earth are they up to?

I do not agree with their assessment. Well, even if they are right, what audacity they have to make fun of me! Can I do anything about it? I have on numerous occasions pleaded with them to stop behaving in that manner, but all my pleas fell on deaf ears.

Today whilst on the street it happened again! "*Big tum, tum!*" (referring to my protruding belly) and "coconut head!" one of them taunted me to the face. I was so infuriated; I lost my temper. In my rage, I got hold of a small stone (they abound on the streets of our little village) and threatened to throw it at the offender. I thought he would heed my warning. But no! Instead of leaving me in peace, he cautioned me even further. I am very sorry to report this, but then I lost my temper and did what I shouldn't have done—namely aim the stone at him! Sensing danger, he took to his heels and began running away. Too late! The stone hit him on the upper back. I thought he was going to retaliate, but he didn't. Instead, he went away crying at the top of his voice.

The incident was witnessed by an adult who happened to be walking past.

"Why did you do that to your friend?"

"You mind your own business!"

"Hey, who taught you to be so rude?"

"Didn't I ask you to mind your own business?"

He wouldn't take anything of that and charged toward me, his right arm raised... to give me a knock on the head? Or slap me, perhaps?

Sensing danger, I took to my heels and ran away as fast as my legs would carry me.

Kwaku was the first to see me on my arrival. He noticed how I was panting for breath.

"What is the matter, my friend?"

"Stop being nosy!" I retorted.

"Well, I hope everything is fine with you?"

"I'm okay," I sulked, "Nothing to worry about.

*

I thought that was the end of the matter. It wasn't. Not long after my return, Father arrived. After greeting everyone, he unexpectedly got hold of me.

Quickly, he urged Mother to fetch some ginger. Next, he asked her to crush it in a stone crucible. She was told not to crush it into power, but rather to leave it in a semi-solid state. Next, he asked Kwaku and Kwabena, who happened to be on holiday, to assist him and restrain me. He then gave Mother the signal to proceed! Mother then quickly pulled down my slip, removed part of the ginger paste, forming it into the shape of a suppository, and inserted it into my back door! Soon I could feel the terrible hot sensation in my back passage!

As I wailed at the top of my voice I could hear Kwaku's teasing comments: "That hopefully will teach the rude fellow a lesson in good manners!"

I am used to Kwame's ridicule; but the realisation that Kwaku would send a jibe in my direction at a moment when I needed his solidarity came as a real shock!

3D

EAR- SPLITTING BUM TRUMPETS

So far I have been sleeping with my parents. As already mentioned, initially I was sleeping on the bed of my parents. But after the birth of my sister I lost my favourable position on the bed of my parents. Instead, a mat, not a mattress, was spread in front of their bed. It was fairly well cushioned using bed sheets, which made sleeping quite comfortable.

I thought the situation would persist indefinitely. I was wrong.

One day, Mother unexpectedly turned to me and began:

"Kofi, from tonight onwards, you will be sleeping with your brothers!"

"No, I am scared to sleep with them!"

"No, you are not!"

"What will happen if I need to open my bowels in the night!"

"When was the last time you had the need to do so?"

"I don't remember!"

"That is the reason we have decided you can now share the room with your brothers. You were indeed able to keep dry throughout the night. The only problem is you occasionally wet your bed. That is to be expected. I am confident you will be completely dry in the very near future though."

"Still, I am scared. What happens if I have the urge to open my bowels one night?"

"You can awaken Kwaku from sleep and ask him for help!"

"Awaken me from sleep!" Kwaku interjected. "Don't you dare, my brother!"

"That is exactly what you did when you were of his age. You were helped by Kwabena; now it is your turn to help him!"

"I am happy to help him so long as I am awake. He should however not dare awaken me from sweet sleep!"

*

Mother has put her words into action. It is now nightfall. I am now sleeping in the boys' room. There is no bed in our room. We are sleeping on mats spread on the floor. Kwaku is sleeping next to the wall, Kwame is in the middle, I am sleeping farthest from the wall and nearest to the door.

I have over several months also been sleeping on a mat spread in front of the wooden bed of my parents—not a mattress, I must stress. It was quite comfortable though because two bedsheets were spread on the mat to provide a kind of cushion. Not in this case, though. This is really hard stuff—sleeping on the bare mat spread on the hard cemented floor!

As mentioned elsewhere, there is no electricity in our village. At night our household makes use of two Swiss kerosene lamps to lighten our home. When retiring to bed, one of the lamps is assigned to each room. Kwame and Kwame made me understand that it was their custom to turn off the light while sleeping since it disturbed their sleep. I objected to the idea, citing my fear of the dark. In the end a compromise was reached. The flame will be turned very low instead of being put out completely.

Poor me! Our lamp has run out of fuel—and on the very first night of the new sleeping arrangement! It was an oversight on Mother's part. Kwaku has made it clear to me. According to him Mother usually ensures there is at least a half-full bottle of kerosene for emergency use. It is now too late for her to intervene—she has already left to sleep in Father's extended family home. So, we have to do without any light in our room. It is dark, really dark in the room! I am scared to death! I have pushed up close to Kwame who is sleeping nearest to me—as a way of overcoming my fear.

216

I don't want to draw attention to the sizzling sound of the mosquitoes! It has become part of night life—whether in Father's room or in this, there is virtually no difference. For now we are spared the noises from the frogs and the owls—the question though is for how long.

*

I really wish sleep would come to me, but as it appears it doesn't care. Is it because of the change from my parents' bedroom to this? Whatever the reason, I am really struggling to sleep! I am turning and turning on the hard surface!

Hey! That was an ear-splitting noise!

"Hello, who is threatening to shake the foundation of the building with such explosive flatulence?"

No response.

The air was released not only with a bang from the tummy of the individual involved, it is also foul smelling. I am not sure from which of the two other humans in the room it originated from. In my opinion, whoever it came from should head straight to the community latrine to empty his bowels!

*

I don't know how long I was lost in sleep. The fact remains that I have been awakened, not gently but rather violently, by Kwame who sleeps just beside me. He definitely did not mean to hurt me. As already stated, this is the first time I am sharing a room with both brothers. Though it is too early to draw conclusions, based on what I have observed and been victim to, he seems to be a wild sleeper, someone who sleeps with one eye open.

Yes indeed, just as I was lost in sleep, suddenly I felt as if I was being pushed aside with the help of a solid object. On waking up, I noticed I was no longer lying on the mat, but rather on the bare cement floor. Kwame was lying beside me, half of his body still on the mat, the other half on the floor.

As I came back to myself, Kwame who was still lost in sleep kept pushing me using his elbow.

"Stop pushing, Kwame!" I cried at the top of my voice.

If I expected a response from him, I was disappointed, for he was still deeply lost in sleep. Fortunately, Kwaku was awake. Noticing what was going on, he helped pull Kwame back to his original position, thereby helping to create space for me.

I was so tired that sleep soon took hold of me. When I awoke in the morning, I was lying nowhere near the mat, but rather quite a distance away. Thus my first night of sleep with my brothers came to an end.

3E

A FUTILE LAST-MINUTE DASH FOR A COMMUNITY LATRINE

This is exactly what I had feared when Mother announced I was going to sleep with my brothers! Well, the first several days passed without any incident involving the need to go to the toilet during the night. Not so last night!

Was it the urge to open my bowels that threw me out of bed, or did I just awake from sleep only to feel the urge to do so? Whatever the case, I woke up in the night with an urgent feeling to open my bowels.

The male community latrine is at the other end of the village. It is superfluous to state that I couldn't imagine going there alone! There was thus no option left than to wake Kwaku from sleep. As expected, he was not amused at the prospect of stepping out into the dark.

Despite the odd-hour disruption of his sleep and also the fact that I am not always the nicest brother to him, his sense of duty and feeling of responsibility towards his little brother without doubt took precedence over everything else! "Come along, my dear little one." Thus he encouraged me, as he turned up the flame of the lamp. It was a particularly dark night—we would hardly have found our way without it. I hurried along the streets of the little settlement, my brother walking alongside me. About midway through our journey, the pressure to open my bowels grew stronger and stronger. I did my best to suppress the compulsion—to no avail, as it turned out!

Just as we were about twenty metres away from our destination, it happened—everything rushed out of my body like water! It is superfluous to mention here that we aborted our journey and returned home. On getting back home, Kwaku, bless him, helped me clean myself.

I have only one set of clothes, with nothing to spare. If Mother had been around, she would without doubt have given me one of her clothing items for the night. Since that was not the case, I had to return to sleep wearing nothing—a situation that no doubt came as a delight for the mosquitoes who seized on the opportunity to suck as much blood as they could from my completely exposed body.

When Mama learnt what had happened in the night, she was all-praise for Kwaku.

"You deserve an egg for your lovingkindness to your brother," she smiled at him.

"Me too!" Kwame cried aloud!

"What contribution did you make? Weren't you asleep the whole time?" Kwaku shouted.

In the end Mother cooked five eggs for the three of us, herself and Papa.

*

3F

JUST WHO IS RESPONSIBLE FOR DISCIPLINING CHILDREN?

I thought the correction of misbehaving children is the remit of only their parents and close relations. Well, that doesn't seem to be the case in our community, judging from what I'm about to narrate here.

As I was playing with my playmate Kwesi on the street a small misunderstanding developed between us. In the end we were engaged in a scuffle. In my opinion, it was a minor fuss between good friends. We could indeed have resolved the matter on our own. But an adult who happened to be passing by thought otherwise. On seeing what was happening he turned to us and began:

"Hey boys, you better behave yourselves or I'll show you the red!"

"Mind your own business, Sir!" we cried as if with one voice.

"Hey, boys, didn't your parents teach you good manners!"

"Yes, they did."

"Why then are you being insolent to me?"

"We are not insolent; we just wanted you to know that what's happening between us has nothing to do with an adult!"

"You shut up!" he roared at us.

Without any warning, he got hold of a small cane that happened to be lying around and with it began lashing us!

Kwesi and I took to our heels and ran as fast as our legs could carry us. The stranger pursued us for a short while before giving up. In all I received a couple of lashes to my body.

On getting home I reported the matter to Mother. To my surprise she did not find anything wrong with the behaviour of the stranger.

"You've got to behave yourself wherever you go if you are to avoid a repetition of such incidents in the future," she cautioned me.

I still don't get it! What type of community is this, a society in which strangers, indeed individuals I bear no relation to, see it as their duty to interfere with my life!

YEAR 4

4A

ANIMATED CHATTING BETWEEN TWO COUSINS

Today is my fourth birthday!

Actually, I do not possess a birth certificate. Father never attended school. I am sure he would have been a good student. In any case, according to him, he learnt the art of writing from his playmate. He tells us he can count up to a hundred and also write fairly legibly. In the end he acquired a notebook and recorded all the dates of births of his children.

As I mentioned on a previous occasion, marking birthdays doesn't seem to be part and parcel of the culture of the society I have elected to visit.

*

The other day I was playing with Aya, a cousin of mine who lives in our district capital Akim Oda. She happened to be visiting the village with her parents, and she mentioned that she usually throws a party for her classmates on her birthday.

"Throw a party? What do you mean by that?" I probed further.

"You don't understand that?"

"I wouldn't have asked if I knew, my sweet cousin!"

"Okay, pay attention as I explain. my dear. This is what happens. On my birthday, Papa and Mama purchased several pieces of cake, biscuits and other confectionery—enough to go round my twenty-five or so friends. Besides the sweets, they also supply everyone with soft drinks."

"Soft drinks? What do you mean by that? There are no hard drinks around, are there?"

"Oh no! So you haven't ever heard of the term *soft drink?*"

"No."

"Examples are Fanta, Coca-Cola, Pepsi-Cola, Sprite, etc."

"No idea. How do they taste?"

"Sweet; really delicious! No worries, next time we are visiting I will bring some along. For my good cousin."

"That is very kind of you."

"Oh, I like you very much. You are indeed my favourite cousin. I will ask Mother if I am allowed to invite you to visit us so you can have a taste of city life!"

"Thank you very much my darling. I only hope my parents can bear the transportation costs."

"Ach, they should be able to do so! My father paid for all five of us to travel here!"

*

Ouch! My dear cousin—she seems to be living on a different planet!

So, I am four years old. What does the future hold for me?

The other day, Aya—ah, who else?!—told me she started attending Kindergarten when she was three years old.

"Kindergarten? What is that?" I inquired.

"You have never heard the name?" she wondered.

"No."

"What about Day Nursery?"

"No idea; are they food for children?"

"Food for children?!" she repeated my words, laughing her head off. Indeed, for a while she couldn't stop laughing!

"What's so funny, my dear?"

"What led you to think Kindergarten and Day Nursery are names of food?"

"It was just me, your cousin, the bush boy guessing!"

"No, they are not food. Kindergarten or Day Nursery are places where children like you and me go to play and learn when they are young."

"Oh, I see! Do you also attend a kindergarten?"

"Yes, of course."

"So you don't accompany your parents to the farm?"

"To a farm? We don't have any farms!"

"So how do you come by your daily meal?"

"Mother buys food from the market!"

"How does your mother find the money to buy food every day?"

"My father works in an office; he earns a lot of money, enough to care for everyone at home!"

"Well, we have to go to the farm almost every day to fetch food. When I asked Mother why, she told me Father has no money to purchase food."

"Ouch! I cannot imagine myself going to a farm on a regular basis. That indeed is the reason I hate accompanying my parents on their visits to the village. A few days ago I accompanied Mother to one of the farms of her older brother, my uncle that is. I might have come into contact with a leaf, a plant or something my skin cannot tolerate. My body has since then not stopped itching. I have vowed to myself—'You, pretty Aya, you are no longer going to step into that damned bush! Do you get it!'"

"Well, I accompany my parents to the farm Mondays to Saturdays. I do so even on some Sundays. I don't know whether my situation will ever change!"

"What a pity, my dear Kofi! You know what?"

"Tell me, darling."

"I will be six next year. I will be starting school. I am really looking forward to it. I want to become a doctor one day!"

"Well, Father tells me I may one day end up like himself—a farmer. I guess he hasn't got the means to pay for our education."

"What a pity. Don't be sad. I will ask Father if he will allow you to stay with us, to give you an opportunity to attend school."

*

On the occasion of my fourth birthday I decided to find out from my parents when I would be going to school, and if it was anytime soon. I will start with Mother.

"Hey, Mama, when will I be going to school?

"Ask your father."

"Hey Papa, when will I be starting school?"

"Why are you asking?"

"I was playing with Aya, my cousin, the daughter of your own sister who is on a holiday here. She told me she has been attending the Day Nursery and that she will be going to school next year!"

"The government has promised to provide education for everyone. When that happens you will be sent to school."

"I don't understand!"

"What don't you understand?"

"Is it not the same government that is providing education for Aya? So if Aya is permitted to go to school, why not Kwame and myself?"

"Everyone is different, my boy. I did not go to school; your mother did not go to school. Aya will be going to school. Let's hope the government keeps their promise so you are also able to attend school."

"I don't understand the logic behind what you are saying."

"Is your father trying to be economical with the truth?" Mother joined in.

"Economical with the truth? What does that mean?" I inquired.

"I think he feels embarrassed to let you know the main reason why Aya is able to start school whilst you are not. The plain truth is that we don't have enough money to pay for your education. Sadly, whereas Aya's parents can afford to pay for her education, we cannot afford to pay for yours. We are hoping for the government to fulfil their promise to provide free and compulsory education to every child of school-going age. That is what they promised when they were fighting for independence. We have been independent for a few years now. Let's hope they keep their promise. When that happens, you will be sent to school without delay. Are you happy with that explanation?"

"Well, I don't understand everything, but I will desist from asking any further questions so as not to prolong matters."

*

My cousin Aya has been telling me so many amazing stories of life at her home which leaves the impression they are living on a different planet. There are so many stories I have even lost count of them. Among others, she talks of water being transported through pipes into their homes! One only has to turn a tap to get the water flowing! No need to walk to a riverside like we do, to fetch water!

She also speaks of them only needing to press a plug built into the wall of their home—and lo and behold light shines from bulbs fixed to the ceilings and side walls of their homes! Aya keeps telling me she cannot stand "the awful scent of the fumes from the swiss kerosene lamps that illuminate homes" in our village.

Still further—she boasts of having her own room, having her own bed, and having access to factory-made toys, which are nothing like the crude hand-crafted car toys we play with here.

Before I end the *roll call* of stories I want to make mention of a gadget she spoke about. According to her the device is built in the shape of a box. The moment it is switched on, pictures of moving objects—humans, houses, trees, vehicles, etc., appear on a screen in front of the device.

"How can I believe such a story!" I asked.

"Why not?"

"It feels like a fairy tale to me."

"No, it is not a fairy tale. It is the truth, the very truth!"

Though she swore on it, doubts still linger in my mind.

Is it not perhaps an invention on her part, a fanciful creation by her to impress her cousin, the village boy?

*

4B

FARMER OR ACADEMIC?
ONLY TIME WILL TELL!

Today I am told it is New Year's Eve. We are being ushered into a new year. From my own calculation a little over ten weeks have elapsed since I turned four. As I stand at the threshold of a new year, I am taking stock of life outside the peaceful enclosure I emerged from a little over four years ago.

What an action-packed four years they have been! From my arduous journey through Mother's womb, to the harsh realities of daily life, it has been a thrilling experience. My parents, in particular Mother, are my heroes, yes my true champions.

Mother! How she manages to keep her composure in the face of the seemingly unending daily problems, challenges, hurdles, etc., is truly remarkable, indeed really astonishing. Father is also amazing. He works incredibly hard, from dawn to dusk, to keep the family above water financially. I really do wish Father and Mother could earn our livelihood through performing less tedious assignments, and not by means of the bone-breaking chores they are forced to engage in on a daily basis.

Despite all the challenges, hindrances, drawbacks, etc., life at home, to my delight, is generally cordial. Of course, it is not a heaven on earth at home. As expected, there are instances when tempers flare up between us. Concerning Papa and Mama it usually revolves around the chronic shortage of money. Happily, tempers cool down after a while and life takes its normal course.

Concerning the latest developments in the lives of my siblings:

Kofi Fosu is heading towards 18. I hear he is about to complete his apprenticeship in tailoring. Father is said to be planning to set up a tailoring workshop for him in the village when he is done with his training. He is a really hard working fellow and I am sure he will be successful in his trade.

Kwabena is the only one attending school in the family. As already mentioned, he comes home only during the holidays.

Kwaku and Kwame are the siblings I interact with on a daily basis. Of course, there are their petty squabbles, skirmishes, arguments, now and again. I don't take those seriously—they can be considered as a natural part of the usual petty rivalry between siblings.

Princess Late is enjoying her special status as the only girl at home. My little sister—we are all proud of her! I guess she appears to feel alone in the company of her five big brothers. I am the one she usually approaches when looking for a playmate. Unfortunately, we have conflicting interests. Whereas I am attracted to the game of football, she always seems to want to play with cooking utensils!

In the end Mother remains her only real buddy.

*

I have not had the courage to find out from Mother in person. I heard Kwaku telling Kwame the other day that she was expecting a baby. It could indeed be the case because I have noticed her tummy becoming bigger and bigger lately.

Yet *another* baby for Mother? Yet more stress? Well, let's wait and see. If indeed she is expecting a baby, it would without doubt be good news for Princess Late—assuming the newcomer turns out to be a girl!

I am looking forward to the years ahead. What does the future hold in store for me? I really do wish that I get an opportunity to attend school. It has been the talk here for a while. As already indicated, they are hoping for the government to make good on the promise of sending every child of school-going age to school. I am really hoping that will be the case.

What if that doesn't happen! With all due respect to my decent, hardworking parents, I really dread the prospect of becoming a full-time peasant farmer! The prospect of having to fell any of those huge trees, the likes of Odum, Mahogany, Owawa, making use of a common axe is daunting to put it mildly!

Well, I am not unconscious of the fact that such matters are beyond my realm of competence to influence. If it turns out that is what Providence has in store for me, I will be left with no choice than to accept my fate and tread the path both my parents have trod, if reluctantly.

I heard Kwaku saying the other day that there is a saying "like father like son!" The other day when we were discussing the prospect of us all ending up as farmers, he told me the only way he could perhaps cope was to marry one of the beautiful girls walking our streets; and just as in the case of our parents, produce many children to assist him on the farm.

"Hey, you are dreaming my friend! Do you think it is easy to produce children?" I remarked.

"Ach, Akosua, our playmate told me it is very easy!" he replied.

" Mother told me the other day not to believe everything that girl tells me. "If there is anything one can associate her with, it is the art of inventing fanciful stories!"

*

I have retired to bed now. There was a bonfire on the street to mark the beginning of the New Year. I am lying on the mat spread on the floor of our room; my two other brothers are still playing in town. Kwaku was telling me he intends to stay up till early in the morning. Will he manage to keep awake throughout the night?

I am not afraid, though. Mother is sleeping in the other room with Princess Late, so if any thieves dare come here, she will surely come to my aid. I am tired. I am retiring to bed. I hope no one comes to disturb me.

So welcome to the New Year, everyone! I wish your dreams and wishes come true.

On my part, it is my wish that the New Year brings clarity about my prospect of attending school—not any ordinary clarity, but a positive clarity; yes, clarity that I will indeed be going to school, if not in the course of this year, then at the latest in the following one!

So goodnight—or better still, good morning! And a hearty welcome to a New Year!

EPILOGUE
UNEXPECTED TURN OF EVENTS

My dream of attending school did indeed materialize a little under two years after the events recorded at the end of this narration. Indeed, barely a year after expressing my fears about the prospect of not getting the chance to attend school, the first post-independence government introduced free and compulsory education for every child of school-going age in the country.

The announcement might have come as a surprise to the local authorities charged with the implementation of the policy in tiny settlements the likes of our little village. In the case of Mpintimpi, there were not a few children of school-going age in the village at the time of the announcement. Some were even heading towards their tenth birthday. Against that background was the fact that there was no building suitable for use as a school.

In the end, the chief of the village placed a room that was being used as a corner shop at the disposal of the school authorities. It had enough space for only a few children. In the end Kwaku who was about 8 years old at that time together with six others just about his age, were enrolled in the makeshift primary school.

A native of the village who had just completed his elementary school elsewhere was recruited to take care of the school.

Kwaku, who appeared settled in his occupation as "apprentice farmer", struggled to come to terms with the new situation. One day as he was sitting in the classroom, he spotted us heading for one of our farms accompanied by our two beloved dogs. (The building serving as their school was on the main street of the village.)

On seeing us, the idea occurred to him to walk out of the class and join us! Taking advantage of the fact that his teacher was writing on the blackboard with his back turned towards the class, he sneaked out of the class. Soon the runaway schoolboy caught up with the rest of the family.

Father was clearly dumbfounded on seeing him.

"What are you seeking here?" he burst out, looking him sternly in the face.

"I want to accompany you to the farm; it is boring at school!"

"For God's sake get back as quickly as you can!" Father screamed at him. "Do you want to see me arrested, prosecuted and sent to prison for preventing you from going to school?"

The truant schoolboy on hearing the strong rebuke from his father, had no choice than to turn back, sobbing uncontrollably as he went.

* * *

The following year it was the turn of Kwame and myself to begin our academic journey. We thought the village school would by then have expanded to accommodate the newcomers.

We were disappointed. The authorities had in the meantime decided against developing the school any further on the grounds the little village did not boast enough children to supply it in the future. Thus the children of the village, including Kwaku and his mates, were asked to attend the school at Nyafoman, a bigger settlement two miles to the north.

As might be expected, Kwaku and his classmates were not delighted at all by the idea. What option did they have, however, but to accept the situation as it was!

My academic journey encountered not a few bumps along the way. The major challenge came when I reached Year 5. Owing to an ailment affecting my left ankle, I was unable to walk to school and was subsequently forced to interrupt my education. After a break that lasted two years, I regained my health and resumed my education.

Later on, my academic journey took me to Oda Secondary School. After a five-year period, I obtained my GCE 'O' Levels in 1976. Next, I travelled to Mfantsipim School in Cape Coast, where I was a student for two years. My studies were awarded with the GCE 'A' Level certificate.

Contrary to my expectations, Providence had it that the little boy who was born under the unsterile conditions of a makeshift bathroom turned into a labour ward, would end his academic journey at the Hannover Medical School in Germany, in December 1992!

Those wishing to read a detailed account of how I managed to make it from my little village of birth all the way to the Hanover Medical School in Germany may read my book *THE CALL THAT CHANGED MY LIFE* or the slightly abridged version *MEDICAL SCHOOL AT LAST.*

END

CPSIA information can be obtained
at www.ICGtesting.com
Printed in the USA
BVHW072144170123
656438BV00012BA/452